How to train your Python

Marzouq Abedur Rahman

ISBN-10: 1721591869
ISBN-13: 978-1721591862

DEDICATION

For dad,
The star of my life.

Contents

Part one.

I think; therefore I am.

- René Descartes

Hello reader!

I welcome you and plead you to take these first steps you are about to take into the realm of programming and wizardry with confidence and flair.

I am Marzouq.

Your guide.

And that's Adam, an old friend of ours, possibly older than the first dinosaur.

Oh well, it's never too late to learn. He works part time inside math textbooks.

And here comes Quasimodo! (⊙‿⊙)ᴶ

Ola! (Wait, was that Spanish?)

Quasimodo is a Frenchman from the past (Back when they first figured out how revolutions work). It seems that he is highly motivated to learn something new to bring back to his newly freed people. So motivated in fact, that he invented a time machine from the scrap baguettes and a couple of half eaten croissants he found in a junkyard. Am I bluffing? Not at all.

I am Marzouq.

And that's...

That's John.

He doesn't do much.

And you! Oh, I am so glad to have someone from my era!

I can already tell I'm going to develop some distaste for you only to realize I see you as my child in the end.

Enter Python.

A high-level programming language with a set of unique features built in that can be used to build anything virtual you can think of.

What would you need to in order tame such a magnificent beast?

- Integrated Development Environment (IDE): Your virtual workplace. This is where most, if not all, of your application building/coding will take place. In this book, we shall be using PyCharm by JetBrains. You may even use any other IDE if you feel more at ease with it.

- The language: You will need to install Python on your workstation before you are able to build with it! Head on to https://www.python.org/downloads and download the appropriate installer for your Operating System (We are using a derivative of Ubuntu). Once you're done downloading, execute it and it will do everything else for you! In this book, we shall be using Python 3.5.

- The mind: Get some tissues ready, this will hurt. A lot.

Once upon a time...

Verily for every new story there should be a world, a space, a canvas on which you will be painting and creating on. Let us set up our own world. How you ask?

Well obviously through magic stuffs my boy!

I think...

Go ahead and start up PyCharm for the first time after you finish installing Python 3.5.

You should be greeted by something like this;

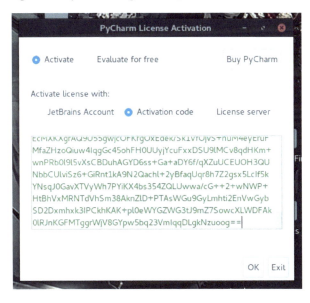

You can obtain a license through either buying one or applying for a free educational license at JetBrains website.

Once upon a time

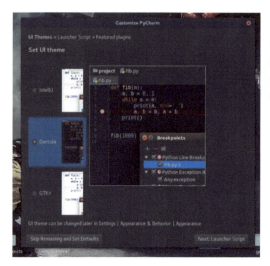

Then you should be taken through some setup, to which you can just leave as default or to your will.

Now, you should create a new project for learning purposes.

Once upon a time

I shall name my project "30days" because I intend to teach you how to code within that time span.

And finally, we shall create our canvas;

The Python file.

This is where all the magic happens.

Right click on the project folder and click on "Python file"

Name it whatever you want

Your first program

Now that you are ready to get your palms greasy, let's just jump right into it.

Let us start this wonderful journey with the infamous line:

```python
print("Hello world!")
```

Go ahead, type that into your IDE and execute it.

Quasimodo, please let John go, we aren't beheading anyone today.

What are you waiting for?!

Oh right... I didn't teach you how to execute your code...

There are two ways. One way is through the IDE as shown below.

That green "play" button is a simple execution of the program you are currently working on. And if you press the bug icon, the program run with a debugger attached to it.

That's all you need to know for now. In this lesson, we shall be using the play button.

The second way is by using the terminal or the command prompt (as referred to in Windows operating systems. The command is just the same so try not to freak out if my junk doesn't look like yours.

First, let's open up the terminal and drop into our working directory by using the command "cd 'directory'" as shown on the left.

Your first program

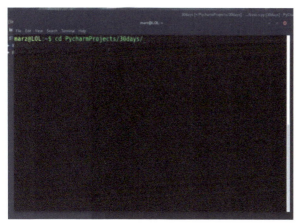

Keep in mind that your directory may be different. Best way to find out is by keeping track of your project directory, with every folder hop denoted with a '/'

Now we shall execute the program with the command "python 'yourprogram.py'" as shown in the next page;

Or add a "-d" flag to debug your program as shown here:

```
python -d basics.py
```

Great. Now that's settled, shall we begin?

Go on, execute your program.

Or don't.   ¯\\(°_o)/¯

Don't look at me, that was all you.

If you didn't make a mistake like your parents did by having you, then the output should be like:

```
/home/marz/.virtualenvs/30days/bin/python /home/marz/PycharmProjects/30days/basics.py
Hello world

Process finished with exit code 0
```

See that "Hello world" text that was spat right back at you?

For the sake of this chapter's discussion, think of the Python interpreter as a mathematically gifted child that does whatever you ask it to do.

Sometimes it throws tantrums with silly and nit-picky reasons.

And other times it behaves **so well** that you will find yourself on the edge of your seat filled with anxiety and questions that goes a little like:

"Why does it work so well?"

"HOW IN THE WORLD DID THAT WORK?!!!???"

And if you ever find yourself in such a state, do not panic, for that is the curse of being a programmer.

However, it might be comforting for you to know that behind every problem lies a simple solution like inserting a missing ":" or fixing a typo. Much like how a toddler may throw tantrums because his morning cereal was poured into his bowl before the milk.

What was that?

No, I wasn't referencing a popular book authored by Jeff Kinney.

MOVING ON.

I think you can already tell that the command "**print()**" was used to display a text on the screen. And if you are not a complete nutcase, then it should also be evident that whatever you put inside the quotations will be regurgitated right back out.

Don't believe me?

┴──┴ ⌒ヽ(`Д´)ﾉ⌒ ┴──┴ WELL TOO BA-

I mean; you can go ahead and try it yourself if you don't believe me. Go on, print out your name, your address, your passwords and your social security number. Oh, and don't forget to send me a copy of all that!

Here's a fun exercise, find out what happens when you add a comma between two quotes as shown below:

```
print("Hello world.","English is not my first language!")
```

Output:

```
Hello world. English is not my first language!
```

Neat isn't it? Flip over to the next page for the next lesson.

Or don't. I'm just words embedded on pieces of paper, you have no obligation to do as I say.

Seriously? Is that what humanity has come to?

Reading pointless sentences to eat away at time?

Suit yourself.

The guideline

Now don't get all cocky and arrogant just because you have written and successfully executed your first piece of code.

Need I to remind you that that was just a single line of code!

But that's why we learn don't we?

First to spell, then to construct a sentence and then later on, a paragraph or two. And if you are the one who bought this book, then chances are that you know how to read.

Therefore, you must be acutely aware of the **various rules** and **styles** to which we must abide by in the English language (or any other language for that to matter) in order to present our ideas and thoughts in a way that is comprehensible for our fellow human beings (Please don't get offended if you identify as an Apache helicopter).

Python, in this way is similar. We must abide by some rules in order to make sure the computer understands the set of instructions you gave.

We do this by abiding to **parameters**, **indentations**, **commenting**, by arranging our lines to either be **single line statements**, **multi-line statements**, or by grouping them together as a **suite**. In time you shall know all the tricks that a Python "master" should have up his sleeve. Careful now, one step at a time.

As of now, commenting and multiple statements in one line are topics of importance for us.

You don't agree?

I couldn't have possibly cared less.

Me> (┌■_■)┐┬┬┬─ (┬﹏┬) <You

Commenting and the lot

Now, **commenting** is easy and straightforward.

```
#This is a comment
print("Hello world!","England is my city.")    #this is also a comment
#it doesn't matter how many times you do it or where you put it
```

Just put a hash-tag anywhere and comment away!

Just try not comment inside the statements, you dense nut.

Comments are useful to keep track of what is going on and to write reminders to your future self (or to fellow programmers!).

Execute the code above and you shall observe that the **comment**(s) will be ignored by the Python interpreter, just like you were ignored as a child.

Poor thing...

(づ｡◕‿‿◕｡)づ

ANYWAYS;

To squeeze multiple statements in one line, simply insert a semicolon at the end of the first and corresponding statements as shown below:

```
print("Hi");print("This is a multi-statement line");print("Isn't this fun?")
```

Go ahead, execute that. Is your mind blown yet?

My sincere apologies if that was as boring and uninteresting as your life.

Planning

We now move on to the part of the book that would teach you a crucial step to take before taking on a large project.

The first part to any journey it to plan and chalk out an outline.

Kind of like writing an essay, you have to sketch a diagram to describe the intro, climax and ending.

For some, it is an absolute necessity to do so whilst others can just spawn masterpieces spontaneously.

Programming gets a bit more complicated than that.

You will want to chalk out an outline for three major reasons:

1) If you are working with someone else, they need to know what you are trying to achieve in each step. Otherwise there will be misunderstandings and it will be very hard to understand each other's segments of code indeed.

2) If you normally take long breaks while working on major projects, then you will find yourself lost in the forgotten thoughts and visions of your past self.

3) So, you can easily identify the possible limitations of your program without needing to scroll through thousands of lines of code.

The most common way of planning is by constructing a flowchart.

You may already be familiar with the graphical representation of code through basic shapes and flow lines. Flow charts don't have actual lines of code in them, instead, they describe their function through a text box embedded in its relevant shape.

Planning

Here are some of the basic elements to get you started:

Shape	Function
	Terminal Denotes the start or end of a program.
	Process Can be mathematical or method operations.
	I/O block Denotes an output or input process like print() or input()
	Decision Shows a decision-making section. Usually ends with several flow lines exiting it depending on the decision. Yes or no being the most common two exiting flow lines.
	Flow lines Shows the direction in which the flowchart is being executed.
	Predefined function A group of statements (usually a user defined function) carrying out an operation.

Planning

Some other elements include:

circle	**Continuation point** Connects another page to the current by acting as the continuation point.
triangle	**Continue point** Denotes the end of the page and that the next is the continuation of this given that a continuation point exists there.

The diagram below shows a simple example of a flowchart by utilizing the element discussed previously.

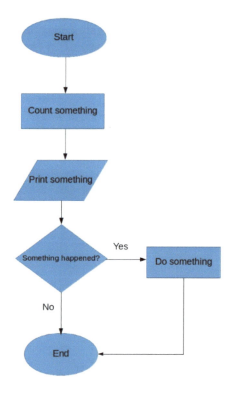

Variables and Datatypes

Variables basically operate as storage units for different types of data. This ranges from simple integer types like 69 to float types like 3.14 all the way up to file types that as you can imagine are a big jump. The names we assign to these variables are called identifiers, they are basically names, but one can guess that the massive nerd behind all this thought it sounded cooler if it was called "identifiers".

Idiot.

I'm joking, please don't edit this out Mr. Editor.

Below is an example of how variables are assigned and how we can use them.

```
y = 69    # y is an integer
pi = 3.14    # pi is a float
1My name = "Sad BOII"    # 1My name is a string

a = b = c = 48    # this statement assign 100 to c, b and a.

print(1My name)
print(a);print(y)
```

Go ahead, execute that.

What's that? It's not working?

A problem with line 3 you say?

Allow me to take a look.

Oh.

Oh no.

It seems that I have made a grave mistake, two to be exact.

You see, identifiers cannot have digits in the beginning of their name (and it should go without saying that identifiers cannot be integers), they only accept underscores or letters of the English lexicon as the first character of the identifier and simply cannot tolerate white spaces " " anywhere in the identifier.

Racists. What's so wrong about being white?

Why don't you try fixing it?

Too lazy? Do you really need to be spoon fed everything?

You know, this is exactly why obesity is a problem in our society nowadays.

```
y = 69   # y is an integer
pi = 3.14   # pi is a float
My_name1 = "Sad BOII"   # My_name1 is a string

a = b = c = 48   # this statement assign 100 to c, b and a.

print(My_name1)
print(a);print(y)
```

There, that wasn't so hard now, was it? Go on, play around with the code. Execute it (Put that guillotine down, Quasimodo) and savor it.

Input

Chances are that you will want to receive input from the user and put it into a variable.

Don't fret little one (or big one, please stop eating so much), for the function input() is here to save the day.

```
My_name = input("What's your name? ")   # My_name is a string
print("Hi", My_name)
```

Go on, try it out. Getting interesting now, isn't it?

Since you've come this far, I reckon it is time to celebrate with experimenting! Try printing out ages and do math (Don't do meth though) … Basically you can start by testing your ground with your newly acquired knowledge!

Don't be afraid to break the rules and test the limits! Here's a little template for you:

```
name = input("Your name:")
x = int(input("Value of x: ")) # specify data type as integer with the int(input()) encasing.
y = int(input("Value of y: ")) # more of this will be covered in later chapters.
z = x + y
print("Hi", name, ",", "The sum of x and y is", z)
```

That wasn't so bad now was it?

I liked it.

No, I don't like you.

Output

I think that you would agree that outputs are very important in programming. Otherwise, there is no real reason to create the program if it doesn't create a result of some sort.

Now, there are many ways to create outputs. But for today, we shall be talking about screen outputs.

I think you are quite familiar with that.

That's right. It's the print() function.

Well, not entirely, but more of that later.

If you can recall the first little program we executed yesterday was a simple print("Hi) program. Let's talk about that.

Say you want to create a program that prints out something like "Hi Adam!". You might do something like this:

```
name = input("What is your name, trainer?    ")
print("Welcome to Earth", name, "!")
```

You will soon realize that although the program gets the job done, the code is clunky, messy and the output is anything but neat.

```
What is your name, trainer? Reader

Welcome to earth, Reader!
```

Output

In order to organize the code and to create a more tolerable output, we add {} inside the quotations to define the position of the variable, and write down the variables we want to print out (in order or in repetition if the output is as desired) inside a .format() function placed after the ending quote like so:

```python
name = input("What is your name, Python trainer? ")
trainer_id = int(696969)
print("Welcome to Earth, Trainer {}! Your trainer ID is
#{}".format(name,trainer_id))
```

Before we move on to the next topic, let us talk a bit more about the .format() function and how we can manipulate it.

Take the following piece of code:

```python
print('I love to eat {} and {} for breakfast!'.format("beef bacon", "eggs"))
```

Looks simple, doesn't it? When you execute it, all it outputs is a measly;

```
I love to eat eggs and beef bacon for breakfast!
```

But what if we did this?

```python
print('I love to eat {0} and {1} for breakfast!'.format("beef bacon", "eggs"))
```

Go on, try it out.

Same thing? That's to be expected.

Now let's try this:

```python
print('I love to eat {1} and {0} for breakfast!'.format("beef bacon", "eggs"))
```

Now If we were to execute this, then we would get something similar to:

```
marz@LOL:~/PycharmProjects/30days$ python basics.py
I love to eat eggs and beef bacon for breakfast!
```

Output

The word "eggs" gets printed out first instead of "beef bacon". This is because your python has given the strings "names" by counting them from 0. Don't want to degrade beef bacon as a 0?

No worries, just do as I do:

```
print('I love to eat {food} and {0} for breakfast!'.format('eggs', food ='beef bacon'))
```

Specify the identifier inside the curly braces. And as per usual, Python will label "eggs" with a 0. Unless you do something about it of course.

Now, most of the times, you don't need your screen to fill up numbers going up to the 14th decimal place. Adding a ":" inside the curly braces will display the number all the way up to the decimal place you determine.

The example below takes an angle and displays its sine value to 3 decimal places:

```
import math
theta = float(input("What's your angle in degrees?"))
print('The sine of the entered value is {0:.3f}'.format(math.sin(theta)))
```

The f inside the {0:.3f} tells the language that it is a float.

But what happens if we do the same with a integer? Well for one, integers do not have decimal places. But if we were to do as so:

```
theta = int(30)
print('{0:10d}'.format(theta))
```

An interesting output will be produced.

```
marz@LOL:~/PycharmProjects/30days$ python basics.py
        30.
```

And if you adjust the 10, you will find that the space will also be adjusted.

This will become extremely useful in places where you might have to create tables with consistent spacing.

Modules

At times you may need to use more and more functions/variables/ when you are programming, perhaps you want the accurate value of pi but your brain is too lazy to start chanting the numbers all the way up to the 14th decimal place. In this case, we will have to import the "math" module so we can access the related functions.

How is it done? Take a look below:

```
import math
print(math.pi)
```

Execute the program and you shall see that the value of pi will be printed out all the way up to the 14th decimal place. Also notice that to access pi, we had to first type in the module's name followed by a point in order to get to the functions. Think of the module like a folder containing mini programs, first you specify which folders you want in your application, then you pick the programs that come with it.

Go ahead and experiment with the different variables and functions that come with it like the math.sin() function. The sky is the limit.

Getting bored? Math isn't exactly your thing? Worry not little one for there are many more modules to import and play around with.

Don't believe me? You should really stop doubting a book. It's quite unhealthy.

Anyways, if you would like proof, go on and head over to your terminal/command prompt and type in python to drop into the "python shell".

If else statements

This is basically the interpreter where you can explore and work with python in an enclosed environment. But more on that later!

Go on an type in help() for the interactive help then enter in the search word "modules" to get the list of modules available for importing.

Ready?

It's quite a handful isn't it?

```
Help on built-in module math:

NAME
    math

FILE
    (built-in)

DESCRIPTION
    This module is always available.  It provides access to the
    mathematical functions defined by the C standard.

FUNCTIONS
    acos(...)
        acos(x)

        Return the arc cosine (measured in radians) of x.

    acosh(...)
        acosh(x)

        Return the inverse hyperbolic cosine of x.

    asin(...)
        asin(x)

        Return the arc sine (measured in radians) of x.

    asinh(...)
        asinh(x)

        Return the inverse hyperbolic sine of x.

    atan(...)
        atan(x)

        Return the arc tangent (measured in radians) of x.
```

If you would like to learn more about a specific module and its functions/variables, just enter the name of the module and everything you need to know will be listed down.

Operators

You may sometimes have the urge to do your math homework on Python like a glorified hipster.

Why not? As long as it keeps you away from posting narcissistic pictures on social media, I'll be happy to show you how to do so.

Carrying out math operations in Python is fairly simple and often very fast and accurate unless you don't know how to type, or your computer is running on potato power.

Even if your computer is running on potato power (if you get it to work that is) then I can guarantee you that it can calculate 12 to the power of 3 faster than your brain can think about flapjacks.

Arithmetic operators in python

Operator	Description	Example
+ Addition	Adds values on either side of the operator.	a + b = 30
− Subtraction	Subtracts right hand operand from left hand operand.	a − b = −10
* Multiplication	Multiplies values on either side of the operator	a * b = 200
/ Division	Divides left hand operand by right hand operand	b / a = 2

% Modulus	Divides left hand operand by right hand operand and returns remainder	b % a = 0
** Exponent	Performs exponential (power) calculation on operators	a**b =10 to the power 20
//	Floor Division - The division of operands where the result is the quotient in which the digits after the decimal point are removed. But if one of the operands is negative, the result is floored, i.e., rounded away from zero (towards negative infinity) -	9//2 = 4 and 9.0//2.0 = 4.0, -11//3 = -4, - 11.0//3 = -4.0

Comparison operators

Then we have the **comparison operators**, which as the name suggests, compares two the value of any two objects. They are as shown below:

Operator	Description	Example
==	If the values of two operands are equal, then the condition becomes true.	(a == b) is not true.
!=	If values of two operands are not equal, then condition becomes true.	(a != b) is true.
<>	If values of two operands are not equal, then condition becomes true.	(a <> b) is true. This is similar to != operator.

>	If the value of left operand is greater than the value of right operand, then condition becomes true.	(a > b) is not true.
<	If the value of left operand is less than the value of right operand, then condition becomes true.	(a < b) is true.
>=	If the value of left operand is greater than or equal to the value of right operand, then condition becomes true.	(a >= b) is not true.
<=	If the value of left operand is less than or equal to the value of right operand, then condition becomes true.	(a <= b) is true.

Augmented assignment operators

And lastly for today's math related lesson, we have the **augmented assignment operators** which is basically the same thing as the traditional assignment operators but written in short form.

...

Why not, eh?

Operator	Description	Example
=	Assigns values from right side operands to left side operand	c = a + b assigns value of a + b into c
+= Add AND	It adds right operand to the left operand and assign the result to left operand	c += a is equivalent to c = c + a
−= Subtract AND	It subtracts right operand from the left operand and assign the result to left operand	c −= a is equivalent to c = c − a
*= Multiply AND	It multiplies right operand with the left operand and assign the result to left operand	c *= a is equivalent to c = c * a
/= Divide AND	It divides left operand with the right operand and assign the result to left operand	c /= a is equivalent to c = c / ac /= a is equivalent to c = c / a
%= Modulus AND	It takes modulus using two operands and assign the result to left operand	c %= a is equivalent to c = c % a

**= Exponent AND	Performs exponential (power) calculation on operators and assign value to the left operand	c **= a is equivalent to c = c ** a
//= Floor Division	It performs floor division on operators and assign value to the left operand	c //= a is equivalent to c = c // a

But wait! There's more!

Do bear with me, I promise there are only two more operator types we have to learn before doing anything fun.

Caught your breath yet?

Let's do this.

Membership operators

Membership operators are basically functions to check if the variable is present in a given data group.

Operator	Description	Example
in	Evaluates to true if it finds a variable in the specified sequence and false otherwise.	x in y, here in results in a 1 if x is a member of sequence y.
not in	Evaluates to true if it does not find a variable in the specified sequence and false otherwise.	x not in y, here not in results in a 1 if x is not a member of sequence y.

Identity operators

Then there are the **identity operators** which checks and compares if two variables are the same thing or if they are not.

Operator	Description	Example
is	Evaluates to true if the variables on either side of the operator point to the same object and false otherwise.	x is y, here is results in 1 if id(x) equals id(y).
is not	Evaluates to false if the variables on either side of the operator point to the	x is not y, here is not results in 1 if id(x)

	same object and true otherwise.	is not equal to id(y).

Still with me?

Great.

If you lost track of something, don't worry, go back read this section again.

Yes, you can do that.

It's a thing called a "book".

Amazing isn't it?

Now for some fun.

Did it occur to you that your Python has yet to be named?

I call mine Bob.

For-

Reasons...

Go ahead, name yours. Choose wisely.

Or not, it's just a Python after all.

Done?

What did you name it?

Really?

That's so unoriginal.

We're on the internet, everything about it is unoriginal.

Murphy's Quantum Law: Whatever **can** happen **will** happen.

If else statements

```
weight = float(input("How many kilos does your suitcase weigh? "))

if weight => 100:
    print("WHAT ARE THOOOSSEEEEEE?!!?!")
    print("What do you mean the meme is dead?")
elif weight => 50:
    print("There is a $25 charge for luggage that heavy.")
    print("Thank you for your business!")
else:
    print("You're good to go!")
    print("Thank you for your business!")
```

Take a close look at the code above.

It's quite straightforward, no?

First, we encase the input with the data type of variable "weight". (That's a float, yes.)

Then we give Bob some directions.

If the weight is more than or equal to 100, he will print out the corresponding **suite** of statements.

Then we tell him that there is another rule he can check if the if statement wasn't true, and that is to check if the weight is more than or equal to 50.

Else, if everything fails, Bob is told to print out the last two statements.

There are a few philosophies you should keep in mind when using if else statements:

- There can be any number of **if** statements, **elif** statements but only **one** **else** statement in the of checks.

If else statements

    - **If** statements will always be checked. This means that regardless of the success or failure of the first/first **if** statement, the corresponding **if** statements will also be checked and executed **if** found to be true.

    - **Elif** statements is an alternate statement and will only be checked if the previous **if/elif** statement(s) has failed. Once the suite gets executed, the remaining **elif** statement(s) will be ignored.

    - **Else** statements will only get checked, and if found to be true, executed if all **elif** and **if** statements fail to execute.

    - **Nested** if else statements work and is encouraged for program comprehensibility by the programmer(s). Below is an example of a nested if else statement in another if else statement:

```
weight = float(input("How many pounds does your suitcase weigh? "))

if weight => 50:
    if weight => 100:
        print("WHAT ARE THOOOSSEEEEEE")
        print("What do you mean the meme is dead?")
    else:
        print("There is a $25 charge for luggage that heavy.")
        print("Thank you for your business!")
else:
    if weight > 25:
        print("You may want to remove some things.")
    elif weight <= 25:
        print("You're good to go!")
        print("Thank you for your business!")
```

P.S: You can even nest inside nested if else statements! Theoretically, you may even make an infinite nest! So, knock yourself out.

How are you feeling?

Take another deep breath.

There we go.

Are you up for a challenge?

Come, let's make our first "real" app using our Pythons.

The challenge

Make a program for one of our most prestigious and revered Python trainers, Robin Hood. The program should be capable of calculating the values of x (roots) given a, b and c following the general equation as follows.

$$ax^2 + bx + c = 0$$

A General Quadratic Equation

_____

The program first asks the user to enter his name and his trainer ID.

Then the entered ID and name then shall be verified to be #6759 and "Robin Hood" in order for the program to proceed, otherwise, the program exits.

Once verified, the program asks for values of a, b and c and later calculates x by using the formula:

$$x = \frac{-b \pm \sqrt{b^2 - 4ac}}{2a}$$

The answer and approach

First off, let's start asking the user for his name and ID:

```
name = input("What's your name? ")
ID = int(input("What's your Trainer ID? ")
```

Then we need to compare the inputs with the given data in the question in order to verify as so:

```
if ID != 6759:
    print("Trainer not found!")
    exit()
else:
    if name == "Robin Hood":
        print("Welcome Trainer!")
    else:
        print("Trainer not found!")
        exit()
```

Then we need to ask for the values of a, b and c like so:

```
a = float(input("What is a? "))
b = float(input("What is b? "))
c = float(input("What is c? "))
```

Now when we look at the formula, we find that we have to have a square root in the equation with complex numbers. Therefore, it is best if we import the complex math module:

```
import math
```

And calculate the equation like so:

```
d = (b**2)-(4*a*c)
x1 = (-b + math.sqrt(d))/(2*a)
x2 = (-b - math.sqrt(d))/(2*a)
print("x = {} @ {}".format(x1, x2))
```

Great! Now we've got it all covered and done, our program starts looking a little like:

```
import math

name = input("What's your name? ")
ID = int(input("What's your Trainer ID? "))

if ID != 6759:
    print("Trainer not found!")
    exit()
else:
    if name == "Robin Hood":
        print("Welcome Trainer!")
    else:
        print("Trainer not found!")
        exit()

a = float(input("What is a? "))
b = float(input("What is b? "))
c = float(input("What is c? "))
d = (b**2)-(4*a*c)
x1 = (-b + math.sqrt(d))/(2*a)
x2 = (-b - math.sqrt(d))/(2*a)

print("x = {} @ {}".format(x1, x2))
```

The result when executed:

```
What's your name? Robin Hood
What's your Trainer ID? 6759
Welcome Trainer!
What is a? 12
What is b? 34
What is c? 5
x = -0.15560450413153695 @ -2.6777288292017967
```

Perfect!

…

Or is it?

You see, you will often find yourself rejoicing just because the program seems to have run perfectly.

It feels great doesn't it?

But then-

APPLES.

Wait… That doesn't seem right…

Oh.

Sorry, was copy pasting from a different website. I'm joking if any of you nutcases are filing a lawsuit with the claim that I plagiarized a website to write this book.

Let's start from the top, shall we?
But then- (Queue dramatic music please)

Robin calls you in the middle of the night, screaming into his headset that the program isn't working as you had advertised to him.

If else statements

You then ask for a screen-shot of the output and this is what he sends you:

```
What's your name? Robin Hood
What's your Trainer ID? 6759
Welcome Trainer!
What is a? 12
What is b? 3
What is c? 4
Traceback (most recent call last):
  File "/home/marz/PycharmProjects/30days/basics.py", line 22, in <module
    x1 = (-b + math.sqrt(d))/(2*a)
ValueError: math domain error

Process finished with exit code 1
```

Oh noes.

Shall we just ditch him and leave him to die in the hands of the number ninjas?

Yes, that was always the option.

Oh, it seems that John doesn't want to let a fellow American die.

We have no choice but to help then :(

First, let's do some research. Where **did** we go wrong?

The output points to line 22 which says;

```
x1 = (-b + math.sqrt(d))/(2*a)
```

Let's keep the operations executed in that line for later reference.

Now let's try to figure out why Bob got stuck trying to process Robin's Xs.

```
ValueError: math domain error
```

Try not to philosophize on the possible meanings Bob is trying to tell to us.

This isn't Hamlet nor is it the 19th century (That was a bad century).

Instead, we will search those words up.

Oh, here's another tip:

Forums and discussion threads like the ones in Stack Overflow and GitHub are life savers.

If else statements

If you find yourself in one such forum or thread, you might notice that most programmers encountering this error had squared or logged numbers equal to or less than zero.

That seems to be true in our case as **d** in Robin's case when calculated is -231, which obviously, is a negative number.

This returns an undefined value in mathematics.

What shall we do now?

The best way to solve this, if you are working on something that hasn't been done before, is to solve the problem by hand.

This means you need to be up for learning anything.

Either that or you can keep digging the internet or just search up a similar tool.

But we aren't here to turn you into a copycat now, are we?

And I'm sure you don't have time for that at the moment, so I'll let you in on a little secret:

Quadratic equations will have a complex root if our **d** is less than or equal to 0.

What do we do with this information?

1) We now know that there are complex math involved in here too, therefore we need to import the cmath module alongside the math module.

```
import math
import cmath
```

2) It is highly probable that Robin might also need to calculate noncomplex quadratic equations, therefore it's best if we set up a system where Bob can check if **d** is less than or equal to zero, and **if** that is the case than we use the square root function from the **cmath** module.

```
if d <= 0:
    x1 = (-b + cmath.sqrt(d)) / (2 * a)
    x2 = (-b - cmath.sqrt(d)) / (2 * a)
```

If else statements

```
else:
    x1 = (-b + math.sqrt(d)) / (2 * a)
    x2 = (-b - math.sqrt(d)) / (2 * a)
```

Oh, and let's ease up Robin's eyes by only displaying x to 2 decimal places too.

```
print("x = {:.2f} @ {:.2f}".format(x1, x2))
```

I bet that will put a smile on his face!

Now our program is starting to look a little more robust:

```
import math
import cmath

name = input("What's your name? ")
ID = int(input("What's your Trainer ID? "))

if ID != 6759:
    print("Trainer not found!")
    exit()
else:
    if name == "Robin Hood":
        print("Welcome Trainer!")
    else:
        print("Trainer not found!")
        exit()

a = float(input("What is a? "))
b = float(input("What is b? "))
c = float(input("What is c? "))

d = (b ** 2) - (4 * a * c)
if d <= 0:
    x1 = (-b + cmath.sqrt(d)) / (2 * a)
    x2 = (-b - cmath.sqrt(d)) / (2 * a)

else:
    x1 = (-b + math.sqrt(d)) / (2 * a)
    x2 = (-b - math.sqrt(d)) / (2 * a)

print("x = {:.2f} @ {:.2f}".format(x1, x2))
```

And when executed:

Eureka!

```
What's your name? Robin Hood
What's your Trainer ID? 6759
Welcome Trainer!
What is a? 12
What is b? 3
What is c? 4
x = -0.12+0.56j @ -0.12-0.56j

Process finished with exit code 0
```

We have saved Robin's life! The number ninjas have been bamboozled yet again!

._.)/\(._.

Part two.

I propose to consider the question, 'Can machines think?'

- Alan Turing

"Can a robot write a symphony? Can a robot turn a canvas into a beautiful masterpiece?"

Nothing...

But then a question.

The right question.

"Can you?"

Will Smith (I call him Won't Smith) could do nothing but stare blankly at the seemingly lifeless robot which so bravely questioned our very perception of intelligence in the movie titled "I, Robot".

And a 12-year-old me could do nothing but think about those words as gravely as my childish mind had allowed me to.

What was then the correct measure of intelligence?

Schools measure it by observing our ability to absorb and regurgitate facts from years of education like glorified cows (certified machines). People on the other hand, tend to deem intelligence as the ability to socialize, inspire and order; much like how a group of chimpanzees pick their leader.

Some experts accept intelligence as a flexible object, meaning the ability to do anything efficiently and in a self-inventing way would mean that the subject is intelligent.

Then another question comes to light;

Is humanity then the pinnacle of intelligence? At least here on Earth?

Get your teddy bear, this is about to get real depressing.

Today, we have managed to develop artificial intelligence that solves problems faster than we do.

We have trained these "networks" to detect patterns and objects faster than we do.

One such network has recently beat human geniuses in a Chinese board game called Go without "thinking" much.

And in case you are unaware, Go is a highly sophisticated board game in which it is impossible to beat an opponent with any predetined strategy. This is because the game gets infinitely complex as it progresses with an infinite number of possible moves being unraveled with every single turn.

We have thus proven that we are nothing but pathetic "gods" to soulless slabs of minerals.

And that my dear reader, is the grand failure of humanity.

Think about it in this way;

Say our entire education system was taught with by a language of colors.

Mathematics, science, geography and the lot are all described in this universe through colors.

Now say we have a color-blind child who has the capacity to express and understand those concepts not through colors, **but** through shapes. And if mathematics were to be described using his shapes, a world of possibilities and doors to other innovations would emerge, previously hidden because of the limitations in the color-language.

We can hardly blame the pioneers of education though, because after all, we might as well be cats fascinated by but not understanding of the concept of television, meaning that the answer might be right in front of our eyes, but we are incapable comprehending it.

But this child can. He has the capacity of unlocking mysteries which we are unable to even begin to understand because we can only think in colors and not shapes. But alas, he has failed to understand how the world works through color, thus he is now labeled as a "C-grade" student; incapable of rising among the ranks of geniuses like Newton.

God knows how many of these gifted and intelligent souls much like the child we have described above have been lost and forgotten because of our disgustingly short-sighted education system.

I now ask humanity in entirety; how do we help these hidden geniuses to understand our world in a way they understand but we do not?

And until we find an answer for that, one thing is for certain;

Intelligence does not obey a certain direction of thinking.

And computers certainly don't think like we do.

How a Python thinks

Computers don't think in sentences or visual images.

Instead, everything they do revolves around numbers.

Some numbers are as simple and small as 1 and others as irrational and infinitely large as pi.

All are processed and solved unbelievably fast.

Computers, in that sense, think and speak mathematically.

Thus, anything they do is in forms of mathematical operations, one way or the other.

Programming languages serves as bridges to the incredible numerical world of computers. We do this by converting everything to numbers, so the computer would then be able to make sense of the human realm.

Python as an object-oriented language takes the approach of assigning strings or any other variable to an IDs (a mathematical numeral).

In a nutshell, IDs are the objects to which variables and strings point to.

This means that if A = "Hello" and B = "Hello", then A and B aren't twins, they are both pointing to the object "Hello" which has an ID.

Don't believe me?

Would a little faith kill you?   •`_`•

Fine, let's prove it.

```
A = "Hello"
B = "Hello"
print(id(A))
print(id(B))
```

Here we are extracting the IDs of A and B with the id() function and printing them out simultaneously. The output will quite naturally be:

```
139710227394320
139710227394320
```

Exactly the same isn't it? Now let's change B into "hello" and see if it still points to the same ID.

```
A = "Hello"
B = "Hello"
print(id(A))
print(id(B))
B = "hello"
print(id(B))
```

Which gives us:

```
139952066678544
139952066678544
139952066678488
```

You may now present me with the argument that the method I just showed you is a very flat way for proving that Python is object oriented as variables are not considered as objects.

If that is the case, then you are an experienced programmer and I shall give up my uncomplicated way of explaining things and rebut your argument with these two points:

1) Python doesn't exactly have variables. We call them variables for several reasons, the primary reason being the reference and understand its usage in contrast to other languages.

2) These "variables" are simply keys in a namespace, therefore they may as well as be objects too.

Any data or information you give Python will get assigned to a numerical address pointing to a single "object".

Soon, you may find Java fan boys telling you that Java is an object-oriented programming language too, except in places where it isn't.

And then you will stumble across fan girls claiming that everything in .NET is object oriented.

Which again, is a partial statement.

However, I can assure you that Python is **purely** object oriented.

And that is, in my humble opinion, the beauty of it.

It's almost like art really. Linking two distinct types of thinking.

We are "this" close to achieve the perfect bridge between the both of our worlds.

Data structures

Perhaps the most appealing thing about programming languages is that data can be grouped, processed and presented automatically and seemingly effortlessly.

In the world of programming, this **collection** of data is referred to as **data structures.**

And we have to thank for existing for playing a colossal role in that. Consider them as the behemoths in the grand evolution of computer languages. Most people refer to them as **structures**.

And in this book, we will do so too for the sake of not making things seem too complicated.

Structures, as you might have guessed, are technically just groups of information/data. These single **variables** or **data** are called **elements** or **nodes** when referenced to in relevance to being a member of a structure.

A popular form of structure is an array.

Unfortunately, Python doesn't come with a native inbuilt array structure. Instead we use things like lists, strings, tuples, sets and dictionaries.

All these modules serve different purposes and ultimately have different applications.

Of course, this doesn't mean that Python **can't** have arrays. Simply import the numpy module in which you shall find the array function which is recommended in places where mathematically intensive operations are carried out.

Read about direct access and sequential access online if you are interested in knowing why.

Where were we?

Oh yes.

Lists

Lists are ordered and indexed forms of structures, meaning they have a position (index) and they will retain the position unless the programmer or user changes it him/herself.

Creating a list is straightforward; simply encase your element(s) inside a pair of square **brackets []** with each element separated from each other with a **comma,** like so:

```
integer_list = [1, 2, 3, 4, 5, 6, 7, 8, 9, 10]
float_list = [1.1, 2.2, 3.3, 4.4, 5.5, 6.6, 7.7, 8.8, 9.9, 10.01]
string_list = ['Hello', 'world', '!', 'welcome', 'to', 'my', 'world']
```

Simple isn't it?

Lists can be made up of any data types. They can even be mixed together as shown below:

```
string_list = ['Hello', 'world', '!', 'welcome', 'to', 'my', 1, 'world', 2.0]
```

Neat!

Now in order to pick out a specific element to print it, simply specify its position in the list from left to right with the starting element counted from 0.

For example,; let's say Adam wishes to print out the float 2.0 from the following list:

```
string_list = ['Hello', 'world', '!', 'welcome', 'to', 'my', 1, 'world', 2.0, 'version']
```

There are several ways to achieve this.

First method is perhaps the simplest and can be done like so:

```
print(string_list[8])
```

Which spits out the output:

```
2.0
```

"But I've counted, and it was the 9th element! Why is it then listed as 8?"

If you find yourself asking a similar question, then congratulations.

CONGRATULATIONS FOR NOT PAYING ATTENTION WHEN I SAID YOU ALWAYS COUNT **STRUCTURES** FROM 0. ╭○ʊ益ʊ╮つ ─=≡ΣO))

Honestly, why did you even buy this book?

Oh right, you claim to have undaunted determination.

If that's the case, I tip my hat to you and urge you to continue reading for you **might** be destined for greater things in life.

And if Adam was feeling a bit more adventurous, he could have even used **negative indexing** in order to specify the position from left to right like so:

```
print(string_list[-2])
```

Which again would spit out

```
2.0
```

Consider it like telling your Python (I'm sorry, I forgot it's completely unoriginal name) to print out the nth last element.

You get the idea.

Now, often you will find the need to carry out various operations or manipulations with **lists**. I that you that you would be pleasantly surprised to be informed that Python comes with several amazing functions natively.

Using these functions can as easy as drinking a glass of water.

But you need to access them from the *"list."* module/header.

You can even access them by using the identifier as the "header".

For starters, let's try using the reverse() function:

```
integer_list = [1, 2, 3, 4, 5, 6, 7, 8, 9, 10]
list.reverse(integer_list)
print(integer_list)
```

You will now see that the integer list has now been reversed in position which is proven by the output which should be something like:

```
[10, 9, 8, 7, 6, 5, 4, 3, 2, 1]
```

Let's try another, this time let's try the index() function.

Say we are trying to find the position of the number 4 in our integer list, we might start off with something similar to:

```
integer_list = [1, 2, 3, 4, 5, 6, 7, 8, 9, 10]
integer_list.index(4)
```

But notice that when we execute, all we get are blank output and an abrupt end to the execution of the program.

```
Process finished with exit code 0
```

What did we do wrong?

Let's try and deconstruct what's going on over here.

Try thinking like Bob would. In other words, pretend to be a computationally fast simpleton.

First, we gave it a list of integers named "integer_list".

Then we told it to find the number "4" in that list, and if it did find it, to return its position in the list, which is our index labeled with an integer.

Then...

Nothing.

That's all we told Bob to do.

It doesn't know we want it to print the value out for us to see, or to store the value somewhere so we could use it later.

Thus, we must program in detail. And to do so, we need to first determine our purpose with the obtained index. Is it just to display to the user, meaning there is no use in its value in the future? Or is it needed for whatsoever reason later? Or is it both?

If the index will be of no use to you in the near future, and you simply wish to display it to the user, then it may be best if you go on about writing your code like:

```
integer_list = [1, 2, 3, 4, 5, 6, 7, 8, 9, 10]
print(integer_list.index(4))
```

Which will give us the desired output of:

```
3
```

And if we wish to place it in a text we may also write our code to be:

```
integer_list = [1, 2, 3, 4, 5, 6, 7, 8, 9, 10]
print('The index of number 4 in the list is: {}'.format(integer_list.index(4)))
```

Easy. Simple. Everyone's happy.

Now you try the count function.

Go on.

Don't know where to start?

Don't worry, you're not dumb for not knowing (I didn't say you were smart either, stop smiling).

Often as a programmer, you will find yourself not knowing how to use certain functions because the writer of the book you studied or are studying was too lazy to describe every function in detail.

Allegedly.

Don't sue me please.

I'm just a broke little boy.

In my defense, I'm not here to spoon feed you the details.

I am here to show you how the masters of silicon chips think.

How we do the things we do.

Data structures

As the saying goes;

Give a man a fish and he will eat for a day.

But teach a man to fish and he shall eat for life (That is, if he lives near a large water body... Otherwise he's as good as dead).

And that's what I am here to do.

Let's get to work, shall we?

There are three ways of doing this;

The first way is highly informative and something all programmers are ashamed of admitting.

You've guessed it, Google it. Or **DuckDuckGo** it, it's more suited for the needs of programmers.

Simply head onto your browser and search "*Function Name* python release number"

Then simply pick out any site that seems to explain the function in depth, preferably one with examples.

Videos

Now go onto any of the sites listed on the top of your search and you will find detailed explanations along with examples (most of the time). Below is one such example:

```
arbitrary_list = [2,3,4,5,2,4,5,3,4,5,2]
print(list.count(arbitrary_list,4))
```

And when executed, we get;

```
3
```

All we must do now is to make sense of the code in relation to the output.

For starters, we have a list named "arbitrary_list" and it gets called again in the list.count function before the number 4 is called. This shows that we need to specify two things when using the function;

1) A list.

2) An element/the object's whose occurrence we intend to count.

And sure enough, when we count the number of times '4' appears in the list, we get 3 occurrences.

The second way is much faster but might take some getting used to.

If you are using "smart" IDEs such as PyCharm or Eclipse, then you will be reminded of the perimeters/arguments needed to fill in the function while you are coding like so:

The highlighted text is the argument we are currently typing in.

Splendid! Let's try integrating it into our little program.

Say Adam is given a set of numbers that goes a little like:

1,2,3,43,5,56,35,3,4,45,6,4,2,4,6,6,67,2,3,45,46,42,56,34,6,3456,3,32,543,232,5
6,56,4,234,452,3556

And he is instructed to create a simple program asks the user what number he/she wants to count in the list. It should then show the number of times the number pops up in the list.

Data structures

You try it first.

Oh.
You're done?

...

You sure?
You're lucky books don't have eyes -_-

If you were to make such a program, you would first create a list containing those numbers.

Let's label it "number_list":

```
number_list = [1, 2, 3, 43, 5, 56, 35, 3, 4, 45, 6, 4, 2, 4, 6, 6, 67, 2, 3, 45, 46, 42,
56, 34, 6, 3456, 3, 32,    543, 232, 56, 56, 4, 234, 452, 3556]
```

Now we need to ask the user to input the number for the counting process and assign a variable to store the count:

```
number = int(input("Number to count in the list:"))
occur = list.count(number_list, number)
```

And finally, we print the numbers out in a neat way:

```
print("The number of times '{}' appears is {} times".format(number, occur))
```

Finally, our code looks a little like:

```
number_list = [1, 2, 3, 43, 5, 56, 35, 3, 4, 45, 6, 4, 2, 4, 6, 6, 67, 2, 3, 45, 46, 42,
56, 34, 6, 3456, 3, 32, 543, 232, 56, 56, 4, 234, 452, 3556]
number = int(input("Number to count in the list:"))
occur = list.count(number_list, number)
print("The number of times '{}' appears is {} times".format(number, occur))
```

And when executed, you will get an output similar to:

```
Number to count in the list:3
The number of time '3' appears is 4 times

Process finished with exit code 0
```

Remember how I swore I wouldn't spoon feed you information?

I was lying.

Don't look at me like that! Think of it as a form of negative reinforcement.

Your desperation to learn and laziness to ask for a refund for this book gained you independence from the traditional way of learning (*cough* *cough* Memorization).

Was it manipulative? Maybe a little.

Hotel? Trivago.

Methods

append(list)
 	
Adds another element at the end of the list.
	``` A= [1, 2, 3, 4, 5] A.append(6) print(A) ```
	
	Output:
	
	`[1, 2, 3, 4, 5, 6]`

extend(list)
 	
Adds all elements of one list to another.
	``` A= [1, 2, 3, 4, 5] B = [6, 7, 8, 9, 10] A.extend(B) print(A) ```
	
	Output:
	
	`[1, 2, 3, 4, 5, 6, 7, 8, 9, 10]`

pop(ind)
 	
This removes an element from the list from the given index (ind) and returns it.
	`A = [1, 2, 3, 4, 5]`
	`print(A.pop(2))`
	
	Output:
	
	`3`

insert(ind, obj)
 	
To add an element to the list at the given index. Obj is the element you want to add and ind is the index in which the element is to be placed.
	`A = [1, 2, 3, 4, 5]`
	`A.insert(4, 8)`
	`print(A)`
	
	Output:
	
	`[1, 2, 3, 4, 8, 5]`

remove(ind)
 	
To remove an element based on the given index (ind).
	`A = [1, 2, 3, 4, 5]`
	`A.remove(1)`
	`print(A)`
	
	Output:
	
	`[2, 3, 4, 5]`

count()
 	
To count the number of times a certain element occurs in the list based on the given argument
	`A = [1,2,3,2,2,3,4]`
	`print(A.count(2))`
	
	Output:
	
	`3`

clear()
 	
Removes all elements in the given list.
	`A = [1, 2, 3, 4, 5]`
	`A.clear()`
	`print(A)`
	
	Output:
	
	`None`

reverse()	
| Reverses the order of elements in the list. | ```
A = [1, 2, 3, 4, 5]
A.reverse()
print(A)
```<br><br>Output:<br><br>```
[5, 4, 3, 2, 1]
``` |
| **copy()** | |
| Returns a copy of the list.<br><br>In the beginning you may simply type in B = A if you wanted one set to be a copy of another. This method will only leave B to be dependent of A (That is, if A changes, B will also change). However, if we were to use the copy() method, then we will get an independent copy unaffected by A. | ```
A = [1, 2, 3, 4, 5]
B = A
print(A, B)
A.append(6)
print(A,B)
```<br><br>Output:<br><br>```
[1, 2, 3, 4, 5] [1, 2, 3, 4, 5]
[1, 2, 3, 4, 5, 6] [1, 2, 3, 4, 5, 6]
```<br><br>**However, if;**<br><br>```
A = [1, 2, 3, 4, 5]
B = A.copy()
A.append(6)
print(A, B)
```<br><br>Output:<br><br>```
[1, 2, 3, 4, 5, 6] [1, 2, 3, 4, 5]
``` |
| **index()** | |
| Returns the index of a matched element | ```
A = [1, 2, 3, 4, 5]
print(A.index(3))
```<br><br>Output:<br><br>```
2
``` |

Strings

You might have noticed that any variable with its object surrounded with single quotations (') or a pair of double quotations (") are known classified as a **string** data type.

Like almost any other programming language, strings are **structures** of Unicode characters. They are ordered and indexed, just like lists.

Now, if you are not new to the world of programming, then you should keep in mind that Python does not have a character data type. Well, not entirely.

In order to create a single "character" object, we simply create a string with a single element in the structure like so:

```
a = 'a'

# Our 'character' data type, a, is basically a string with its structure's length being 1
```

Like lists, strings have special operations you can carry out on them and can be accessed from "**str**.*function()*"

Str here is the string you are working with.

For example, if we wanted to count the number of times the letter "L" appears in the string **carrots** which points to the word "HELLO", we apply the function like so:

```
carrots = "HELLO"
print(carrots.count("L"))
```

Which would quite predictably give us:

```
2
```

The name of the string will be the header or the "access point".

Operators

In Python, structures can be manipulated through operators. These operators vary in function, but all share a fundamental concept;

They all provide you with some crucial and basic manipulation, checking and presentation functionality without the need to bring up some hard to remember function.

Operator		
+	**Concentration**: This operator will add two structures together.	A = "Hello " B = "World" print(A+B) Output: Hello World
*	**Repetition**: This will repeat the structure *n* number of times.	A = "Hello " print(A*3) Output: Hello Hello Hello
[]	**slice**: This will "slice" and display one element from the structure given its index.	A = "Hello " print(A[4]) Output: o

[:]	**Range slicing:** This will slice the structure from one index to another.	```A = "Hello"num = [1, 2, 3, 4, 5]print(A[1:3])print(num[1:3])```Output:```el[2, 3]```
in	**Membership**: This operator checks if the object supplied is an element of the structure. If it is an element, then the operator returns true and false otherwise.	```A = "Hello "print("H" in A)```Output:```True```
not in	**Membership**: This operator checks if the object supplied is an element of the structure. If it is an element, then the operator returns true and false otherwise.	```A = "Hello "print("H" not in A)```Output:```False```
R or r	**Raw string:** This will override any escape characters and will display it alongside every other character in the string.	```A = R"Hello\nWorld"print(A)```Output:```Hello\nWorld```

The following table is the list of methods available for strings and their examples.

You can skip them if you wish, as long as you understand how they work and how you should read and understand materials from online sources.

Description (* = Optional) (obj = substring/string/character)

capitalize()	A = "hello"
Will capitalize the first letter of the string.	print(A.capitalize()) Output: Hello

center(width, fill*)	A = "hello"
Will insert a space of characters given a width (an integer) and, if needed, the character needed to fill the space (it is simply a space " " by default.	print(A.center(10, " ")) Output: hello

count(obj, beg*, end*)	
This function will count the number of times the substring in question shows up in the string. Obj is the substring, beginning and ending is in form of indexes and is set as 0 and the end of the string by default respectively.	A = "hello" print(A.count("l", 3)) Output: l Or A = "hello" print(A.count("l")) Output: 2

Data structures

decode(encoding*, error*)
 	
encode(encoding*, error*)
 	
Decoding and encoding is fairly simple. You simply provide the
 	
codec in which you want to encode/decode the string in and the error handler (It can be 'replace', 'ignore' and many more!). Both are optional and set at UTF-8 and strict by default.
	``python
	A = "hello"
	A = A.encode('cp424', 'strict')
	print(A)
	
	A = A.decode('cp424')
	print(A)
	``
	
	Output:
	
	``
	b'\x88\x85\x93\x93\x96'
	hello
	``

endswith(obj, beg*, end*)
 	
Will check if string or substring ends with obj. It has will give out "True" if it ends with obj and "False" if otherwise.
	``python
	A = "hello"
	print(A.endswith("o"))
	print(A.endswith("l", 0, 2))
	``
	
	Output:
	
	``
	True
	False
	``

expandtabs(tab size)
 	
This will expand the tab(s) found in the string. Tab size is the number of tabs you want to expand by. It is set at 8 by default.
	``python
	A = "hel\tlo"
	print(A)
	print(A.expandtabs())
	print(A.expandtabs(16))
	``
	
	Output:
	
	``
	hel lo
	hel lo
	hel lo
	``

find(obj, beg*, end*)
 	
Finds if the object is present in the string as a substring and returns the index of the first find or -1 if otherwise.
	```A = "hello"```
	```print(A.find("e"))```
	
	Output:
	
	```1```

index(obj, beg*, end*)
 	
It's just the same as find() but raises an exception if obj is not found.
	```A = "hello"```
	```print(A.index("i"))```
	```print(A)```
	
	Output:
	
	ValueError: substring not found
	
	Process finished with exit code 1

isalnum()
 	
Will check if the string contains at least 1 character and if all characters are alphanumeric. If they are, the function returns true and false if otherwise.
 	
Non-alphanumeric characters are generally symbols (excluding punctuation symbols) and white spaces.
	```A = "hello world"```
	```B = "Hello1234"```
	```print(A.isalnum())```
	```print(B.isalnum())```
	
	Output:
	
	False
	True

isalpha()	
| Will check if the string contains at least 1 character exist and if all characters are alphabetic. If they are, the function returns true and false if otherwise. | ```
A = "hello"
B = "1234abc"
print(A.isalpha())
print(B.isalpha())

True
False
``` |
| **isdecimal()** | |
| Will check if the string contains at least 1 character and if all characters are decimal characters. If they are, the function returns true and false if otherwise.<br><br>Decimal characters are used to denote integers. | ```
A = "hello"
B = "10"
C = "10.11"
print(A.isdecimal())
print(B.isdecimal())
print(C.isdecimal())
```<br><br>Output:<br><br>```
False
True
False
``` |
| **isdigit()** | |
| Will check and return true if the string contains only digits and false otherwise. | ```
A = "hello"
B = "1234"

print(A.isdigit())
print(B.isdigit())
```<br><br>Output:<br><br>```
False
True
``` |
```

islower() Checks if the string has at least one cased character then returns true if all are lower cased and false if otherwise.	``` A = "hello" print(A.islower()) A = "Hello" print(A.islower()) A = "hELLO" print(A.islower()) ```
	Output: ``` True False False ```
isnumeric() Checks if string contains only numeric characters and returns true if it is and false if otherwise.	``` A = "hello" print(A.isnumeric()) B = "1234" print(B.isnumeric()) B = "1a234" print(B.isnumeric()) ```
	Output: ``` False True False ```

isspace()	
Checks if the string contains only white space (" ") characters then returns true if so and false if otherwise.	``` A = "hello" print(A.isspace()) A = " " print(A.isspace()) A = " Hello" print(A.isspace()) ```
	Output:
	``` False True False ```
istitle() Checks if the string is properly title cased then returns true if so and false if otherwise. Proper title casing in Python means every first letter of every word in a string must be capitalized. **Every other character must be lower cased.**	``` A = "hello world" print(A.istitle()) A = "Hello World" print(A.istitle()) A = "Hello world" print(A.istitle()) ``` Output: ``` False True False ```

isupper()	
Checks if the string has at least one cased character then returns true if all are upper cased and false if otherwise.	```A = "HELLO"
print(A.isupper())
A = "Hello"
print(A.isupper())
A = "hELLO"
print(A.isupper())```
	Output:
	``True
False
False```
join(string)	
This function joins two strings together by inserting a "copy" of the secondary string in front of every substring (**except the last**) of the primary string. Primary and secondary clarified: *str1.function(str2)* Where **str1** is the **primary** string and **str2** is the **secondary** string.	```A = "hello"
B = "1234"
print(A.join(B))
print(B.join(A))
print(A.join("Hi"))```
	Output:
	``1hello2hello3hello4
h1234e123411234l1234o
Hhelloi```

Data structures

len(string) This function returns the length of the given string.	```A = "hello"
B = "1234"
print(len(A))
print(len(B))``` Output: ```5
4```
ljust(width, fill*) This will return a function with trailing white spaces on the right (Or any given characters in the "fill" argument)	```A = "hello"
B = "1234"
print(A.ljust(10, " "))``` Output: ```hello```
lower() This function will convert any upper-case character(s) in a string to lower case.	```A = "heLLo"
print(A.lower())``` Output: ```hello```
lstrip(obj*) This function will remove all white spaces (or any string if obj is given) on the left end of the string.	```A = "666hello666"
print(A)
print(A.lstrip("6"))``` Output: ```666hello666
hello666```

Data structures

maketrans(in, out)
 	
The maketrans() function will create a table given two strings (in and out perimeters) of the **same length** with each substring of the same index in both strings mapped to each other. In order to access this function, you will have to navigate to str.maketrans() where str is the string module.
	``A = "Henlo"
	B = "12345"
	Trans_table = str.maketrans(A, B)
	translate_this = "Why am I still writing this?"
	print(translate_this.translate(Trans_table))```
	
	Output:
	`Why am I sti44 writi3g this?`

translate(table, delete*) The translate() function uses the table (generated by maketrans() or your own dictionary) to translate the string.	

max(string)
 	
This finds the "biggest" alphabet in the string and returns it.
	``A = "BCDEFGHIA"
	print(max(A))```
	
	Output:
	`I`

min(string)
 	
This finds the "smallest" alphabet in the string and returns it.
	``A = "BCDEFGHIA"
	print(min(A))```
	
	Output:
	`A`

replace(old, new, max*)	
This function will replace the **old** object (can be a single character or multiple characters) with a new one (can be a single character or multiple characters). **Max** is the maximum number of occurrences of **old** to be replaced.	``` A = "BBBBBBBBBBBBBBB" A = A.replace("B", "BA", 5) print(A) A = A.replace("BA", " HI") print(A) A = A.replace("B", " ") print(A) ``` Output: ``` BABABABABABBBBBBBBBB HI HI HI HI HIBBBBBBBBBB HI HI HI HI HI ```
rjust(width, fill*)	
This will return a function with trailing white spaces on the left (Or any given characters in the "fill" argument).	``` A = "hello" print(A.rjust(10, " ")) ``` Output: ``` hello ```
rstrip(obj*)	
This function will remove all white spaces (or any string if obj is given) on the left end of the string.	``` A = "666hello666" print(A) print(A.rstrip("6")) ``` Output: ``` 666hello666 666hello ```

split(obj*, max*)	

The split() function is in charge of returning lines separated and distinguished in single apostrophes. It will split white spaces by default but will also split based on strings if supplied in the obj argument. The max argument is the maximum number of times it should split. By default, it is set to -1 which will make the splitting go on forever as long as it finds the **obj** it is required to split.	`A = "Hello    World How Are You?"` `print(A)` `print(A.split())` `print(A.split("e"))` `print(A.split("o", 2))`
	
	 Output:
	
	 `Hello    World How Are You?`
	
	 `['Hello', 'World', 'How', 'Are', 'You?']`
	
	 `['H', 'llo WorldHowAr', 'You?']`
	 `['Hell', ' W', 'rldHowAreYou?']`

splitlines()	

This is very similar to the split() function except it splits the string every time it finds a newline "\n".	`A = "Hello \nWorld \nHow \nAre \nYou?"` `print(A)` `print(A.splitlines())`
	
	 Output:
	
	 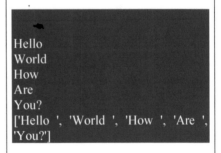 `Hello`
	 `World`
	 `How`
	 `Are`
	 `You?`
	 `['Hello ', 'World ', 'How ', 'Are ', 'You?']`

startswith(obj, beg*, end*)
 	
Determines if the string or the substring (if supplied with beginning and ending indexes) start with obj which is a character then returns true if so and false if otherwise.
	`A = "hello"`
	`print(A.startswith("h"))`
	`print(A.startswith("a"))`
	
	Output:
	
	True
	
	False

strip(obj*)
 	
This is will carry out both lstrip() and rstrip() on the string.
	`A = "666hello666"`
	`print(A.strip("6"))`
	
	Output:
	
	hello

swapcase()
 	
This function will invert all the cases of the letters in the string.
	`A = "hEllo"`
	`print(A.swapcase())`
	
	Output:
	
	HeLlO

title()
 	
Remember title casing? Well start thanking God cause Python has a module to properly title case a string.
 	
P.S: Cool, isn't it?
	`A = "hEnlo hOoMaN"`
	`print(A.title())`
	
	Output:
	
	Henlo Hooman

upper()
 	
As opposed to the lower() function, upper() will convert any lower case alphabet that it finds in the given string into an upper cased alphabet.
	``python
	A = "hEnLo"
	print(A.upper())
	``
	
	Output:
	
	`HENLO`

zfill(width)
 	
This function is fundamentally the same as the rjust() function except it returns the string trailing behind a bunch of zeros depending on the width.
	``python
	A = "hello"
	print(A.zfill(10))
	``
	
	Output:
	
	`00000hello`

Triple Quotation

Maybe you are a fan of Shakespeare and want to store a paragraph from Hamlet and store it inside a string. You may find out sooner or later that it gets exhausting to scroll horizontally as you cram half a page into a single line in your IDE which seemingly stretches to oblivion.

If you are looking to store multiple lines in a string, then triple quotation will be your patron saint.

Before we start I should warn you I am not going to quote Hamlet in here.

You're upset? That's too bad.

```
Triple = """Hello
This is a string
A multi-line string to be more precise.
God, I love triple quotes"""

print(Triple)
```

And as expected, we will get an output similar to:

```
Hello
This is a string
A multi-line string to be more precise.
God, I love triple quotes
```

Tuples

Tuples are very much like lists and strings with the big exception that they are unchangeable, indexed and ordered. This means, tuples cannot be manipulated. In Python we usually denote a tuple using round brackets (). Below is an example of a tuple that stores the names of fruits:

```python
Fruit_tuple = ("Apple", "Banana", "Cherry", "Dragon fruit")
print(Fruit_tuple)
```

And we shall get an output of:

```
('Apple', 'Banana', 'Cherry', 'Dragon fruit')
```

Since we can do anything with tuples but manipulate it, we can use some of the functions we covered in the strings section and apply them here:

```python
Fruit_tuple = ("Apple", "Banana", "Cherry", "Dragon fruit")
print(Fruit_tuple.index("Cherry"))
```

Which gives us:

```
2
```

Sets

Sets and tuples have nothing in common other than the notion that they fall under the structure category. They are the exact opposites of each other with sets being changeable, unordered and unindexed forms of structures.

In Python, sets are denoted with curly brackets {} like so:

```
Fruit_set = {"Apple", "Banana", "Cherry", "Dragon fruit"}
```

And since sets are changeable, we may be able to manipulate its elements but we are not able to carry out any index related process on it since it is unindexed.

Below is one such example:

```
Fruit_set = {"Apple", "Banana", "Cherry", "Dragon fruit"}
Fruit_set.add("Grapes")
print(Fruit_set)
```

And upon execution, we will be seeing something like:

```
{'Apple', 'Banana', 'Grapes', 'Dragon fruit', 'Cherry'}
```

Keep executing and you will find that the order or fruits changes along with every fresh execution (No Quasimodo, no guillotines!), this is because sets are unordered.

Wow.

Did we just finish each other's sentences?
I hope this isn't going to spark something romantic between the both of us.

I'm not blushing. You are. (° ͜ʖ °)

Creep.

Stop staring at me like that...

Dictionaries

Dictionaries are structures that are changeable, unordered and indexed.

In Python they are usually written in curly brackets {} and make use of keys and values:

```
Fruit_dict = {"Apple" : "10",
              "Mango" : "20",
              "Grape" : "30"}
print(Fruit_dict)
```

Which will give us an unordered output of:

```
{'Grape': '30', 'Apple': '10', 'Mango': '20'}
```

Keep in mind that the fruit name here is the key and the number is the value.

Let's say we would like to change the value of one of the keys, we can do so like:

```
Fruit_dict = {"Apple": "10",
              "Mango": "20",
              "Grape": "30"}
Fruit_dict["Mango"] = '50'
print(Fruit_dict)
```

Which will give us:

```
{'Apple': '10', 'Mango': '50', 'Grape': '30'}
```

To add a new entry to the dictionary, we need to add both a key and its value like so:

```
Fruit_dict = {"Apple": "10",
              "Mango": "20",
              "Grape": "30"}
Fruit_dict["Strawberry"] = '50'
print(Fruit_dict)
```

To which we shall get:

```
{'Mango': '20', 'Grape': '30', 'Strawberry': '50', 'Apple': '10'}
```

And if you wish to delete an entry, simply use the del() function and specify the key inside it like so:

```
Fruit_dict = {"Apple": "10",
              "Mango": "20",
              "Grape": "30"}
del(Fruit_dict["Apple"])
print(Fruit_dict)
```

The result:

```
{'Grape': '30', 'Mango': '20'}
```

Constructors

Each of these "structures" can be declared/denoted by their bracket types perimeters. But there is another way to declare and "construct" structures. And it's by using constructors.

Perhaps a table would help your sore brain comprehend the concept easier?

Constructor	Example
list()	num = list((1, 2, 35, 4, 5, 5)) Note the double round brackets.
string()	string = str("hi")
tuple()	tup = tuple(("hi", "Hi")) Note the double round brackets
set()	my_set = set(("apple", "banana")) Note the double brackets.
dict()	my_dict = dict(fruit1="apple", fruit2="banana") print(my_dict) Note that the keys are not surrounded by double quotations whereas the values are.

Ordered, indexed and all that

When using a structure, it is important to be aware of its nature. Is it ordered? Indexed?

By now you might have seen these terms being thrown around like a glorified football. And if you aren't completely worthless, you might be starting to guess what these words mean, in a nutshell at least.

If that's the case, then open the refrigerator and take a bite of that cake you have kept for those lonely little celebrations you so often have now and then.

You like that don't you? (° □ ⟃ °)

HEY!

Try not to spray crumbs all over me. And save some for Adam. Poor dude had to buy 50 watermelons just to have them taken away by some 2nd grader doing her homework. I mean, just look at the state of our education system now. Poor dude buys 50 watermelons for his party and the teacher asks the kid to take away 20.

Indexed: Meaning to have an integer labeled (or assigned) to each element of the structure to denote it's position. It is usually counted from left to right from 0 to the end.

Ordered: This means the structure will have an initial fixed position. Let's say you have a structure containing integers from 1 to 10, coded and arranged in an ascending order. Now, if you were to use an unordered structure to store those numbers, you will find that, upon execution, the numbers have lost their position and 10 may be taking the seat of 2 while 3 is sulking behind 8 (poor thing hates being eaten by 7). You get the point. But if we were to use ordered structures like a list, then this problem wouldn't come to light, all integers are in their happy little places.

Changeable: This should be self-explanatory, but I shall force knowledge down your throat anyways. Changeable here means an element can be added, changed, removed or moved. In other words (for your caveman-ish brains); "IF **CANNOT** CHANGE KRONK **CANNOT** TOUCH."

Data structures

Done? Glad we cleared this up.

I've got something for you.

No. I'm not proposing, you lonely troll.

I can barely kneel!

But you'll thank me for it, I'm sure.

This Venn diagram should aid you in remembering how each structure types work and which methods you can or can't carry out with them.

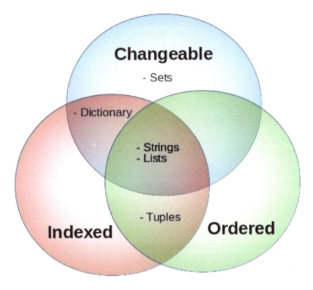

If you are using any third-party structures, feel free to use a pen and slot it into the diagram! Don't worry, I'm just a book, I won't judge.

Fingers crossed though.

Part three.

Whenever the work is itself light, it becomes necessary, in order to economize time, to increase the velocity.

- Charles Babbage

Printing again

Earlier in this book, we learned how to instruct our Python to spit out data in a neat and organized manner.

And now that we have learned data structures, we are ready to learn a bit more in that field.

Say we have a dictionary of names and origins:

```
Peepel = {"Adam": "N/A", "Quasimodo": "French", "John": "American",
"Weird reader person": "Hospital"}
```

How do we print out the origins of Adam and Quasimodo?

You may start off with something similar to:

```
print("Quasimodo: {}    Adam: {}".format(Peepel["Quasimodo"],
Peepel["Adam"]))
```

But what if we didn't want to repeatedly specify the dictionary in the format argument?

If that is our target below is two such ways in which we can achieve our goal:

```
print('Adam: {0[Adam]:}; Quasimodo: {0[Quasimodo]:}:'.format(Peepel))
```

Or

```
print('Adam: {Adam:}; Quasimodo: {Quasimodo:}:'.format(**Peepel)
```

Escape characters

Often times you will find yourself wanting to insert a newline or carry out some other formatting operation within a single print function without having to tediously code some more to achieve the styling or functionality you want.

And boy do I have news for you!

Escape characters are characters that are not printed by default. Each of them has specific roles and are identified with a backslash "\" as shown below:

Escape characters and their functions	
\a	Alerts user
\b	Backspace
\cx	Control-x
\e	Escape
\f	Formfeed
\M-\C-x	Meta-Control-x
\n	Newline
\nnn	Octal notation, where n is in the range 0-7
\r	Carriage return
\s	Space
\t	Tab
\v	Vertical Tab
\x	Character x
\xnn	Hexadecimal notation where n is in the range of 0-9

If you couldn't understand some of them, chances are you don't need them. Not yet at least. But when you do, be sure to come back here, I am a book after all, it's not like I can run from you as much as I'd love to.

User defined functions

You will often find yourself copy a group of statements you have already and reusing them repeatedly in various parts of your program. This in turn makes your source code bulky and messy. And it is in those times you will find yourself wishing for a built-in function to exist that can just imitate your segment of code.

Well, why don't I teach you to code your own functions then?

Let's say I finally allow Quasimodo to use his guillotine to execute his royal Nemesis (R.I.P Yves), then we might want our program to chant "Down with the Kings!" and "LONG LIVE THE REVOLUTION!" along with his deranged self.

We would simply do:

```
print("DOWN WITH THE KINGS")
print("LONG LIVE THE REVOLUTION")
```

But then say Quasimodo starts developing an unhealthy habit of randomly executing anyone he dislikes, and he expects us to chant the two lines every time he does so, what shall we then do when rewriting the two lines repeatedly becomes quite the nuisance?

If you answered, "Stop chanting along with him!" then I must ask you to invite me to your funeral as you are Quasimodo's next target in his gory quest.

What's that? You would abide by his tyrannical command and do as he wishes you to do? Then I'd like to see how you manage to navigate through possibly a thousand redundant lines of code.

DID YOU JUST "FINE" ME!?

HOW DARE YOU! (ノ ° Д °) ノ ︵ /(.□ . \)

Have you forgotten that we are always trying to kill two birds with one stone?

User defined functions

And not only because it is easier to read and write (Although that **is** the main reason), but because it makes the program lightweight, modular and easy to manipulate.

Let's begin.

```python
def chant():
    print("DOWN WITH THE KINGS")
    print("LONG LIVE THE REVOLUTION")
# We are now in the main section of the program
print("This is the start of the program.")
print("Oh look! There goes Quasimodo again (R.I.P John). \nTime to call the function")
chant()
print("Let's carry on with our work.")
print(1+387846735734)
print("Oh no, there goes Adam too :(")
chant()
```

Which if we then *whispers* execute:

```
This is the start of the program.
Oh look! There goes Quasimodo again (R.I.P John).
Time to call the function
DOWN WITH THE KINGS
LONG LIVE THE REVOLUTION
Let's carry on with our work.
387846735735
Oh no, there goes Adam too :(
DOWN WITH THE KINGS
LONG LIVE THE REVOLUTION
```

That was intense.

Now, I think we miss our dead friends dearly.

So, let's make another user defined function in their honor.

User defined functions

```
def cry(string):
    print("Rest in pieces " + string + ".")


# We are now in the main section of the program

name = str(input("Who did Quasimodo kill now?\n"))
cry(name)
```

Here you will find cry() to have an argument or perimeter which we set as a string. "Name" is a string which we will accept as an input from the user and then plug it into the cry() function. We can plug in anything as long as it is a string.

Now let's say we would like to add year of passing into the mix too. In that case, we need to have a multi perimeter function.

```
def cry(string, year1, year2):
    print("Rest in pieces {}.\n{} to {}".format(string, year1, year2))
# We are now in the main section of the program

name = str(input("Who did Quasimodo kill now?"))
birth = int(input("Year of birth? "))
death = int(input("Year of death? "))
cry(name, birth, death)
```

Which gives us:

```
Who did Quasimodo kill now? Adam

Year of birth? 1
Year of death? 2018
Rest in pieces Adam.
1999 to 2018
```

Note that the arguments are arranged in accordance to the perimeter type and name. So, if we were to change the code like:

```
chant(name, death, birth)
```

It will give us:

```
Who did Quasimodo kill now? Adam
Year of birth? 1
Year of death? 2018
Rest in pieces Adam.
2018 to 1999
```

Which would make for a very peculiar tombstone indeed!

We can even call for the function from another Python file by importing it.

Go ahead and create another Python file.

Name it something like my_module.py.

It should contain your user defined function which goes like:

```
def cry(string, year1, year2):
    print("Rest in pieces {}.\n{} to {}" .format(string, year1, year2))
```

And you wish to use that function here in basics.py.

In that case, let us use the from and import statements like so:

```
from my_module import cry

name = str(input("Who did Quasimodo kill now?\n"))
birth = int(input("Year of birth? "))
death = int(input("Year of death? "))
cry(name, birth, death)
```

Execute it and you shall find that it works as expected.

To clarify, the structure of a "from import" statement is basically:

from **python_file_name** *import* **user_defined_function**

Namespaces and scopes

Here's an Easter egg you can check out in Python;

Type in "import this" into the Python interpreter to be greeted by Tim Peters' "Zen of the Python" which is an amazing way to describe the very nature of Python as a programming language. Along the end of the lines, you will read something along the lines of;

"Namespaces are one honking great idea -- let's do more of those!"

So, what are these namespaces?

Remember how everything in Python is an object one way or the other? They all have names don't they (print(), id() and all that)? A namespace in that sense is a place/space in which those names exist collectively, in some cases, they coexist with one another since namespaces typically reside in one another.

Take a look at the following code:

```python
# This is the global namespace
a = 10
def outer_func():
    # This is a local namespace
    a = 20
    print(a)
    def inner_func():
        # This is a nested local namespace
        print(a)
    inner_func()
def outer_func2():
    # This is another local namespace
    print(a)
print(a) # Global namespace
outer_func() # Local namespace
outer_func2() # Another local namespace
```

Namespaces and scopes

The output:

```
10
20
20
10
```

Don't get it? Need a visual representation?

I figured.

Think of namespaces like boxes inside one another.

A box can call up and "see" the object from its parent box but cannot see the object(s) contained within the box that resides within it.

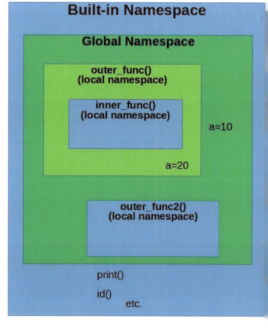

Built-in Namespace

Global Namespace

outer_func()
(local namespace)

inner_func()
(local namespace)

a=10

a=20

outer_func2()
(local namespace)

print()

id()

etc.

Savvy? No?

Here's something for you and Adam;

Smol box **no can** touch

Beeg box **can do a** touch

These "boxes" are called scopes. Smaller boxes are referred to as inner scopes and bigger boxes are referred to as outer scopes.

I hope this topic helps clear up why functions (objects, again) like print() and id() can be accessed from anywhere;

This is because they are from the built-in namespace, the biggest "box" of them all. The mother of boxes.

So, what do you do when you want to let the outer scopes access the objects in their inner scopes?

Namespaces and scopes

There are two ways;

Global statements

Consider the following block of code:

```python
def outer_func():
    def inner_func():
        # This is a nested local namespace
        global a
        a = 30
    inner_func()
    print(a)
def outer_func2():
    # This is another local namespace
    print(a)
outer_func()    # Local Namespace
print(a)    # Global namespace
outer_func2()    # Another local namespace
```

The output you will get will most possibly be:

```
30
30
30
```

The global a statement serves as a mapping. "a", although declared first in an inner scope is not a localized variable.

It is a global variable.

In a nutshell, "a" is now a part of the Global namespace and not the outer_func() namespace. Therefore, any inner scope or "smol box" will be able to access "a" since it is part of its parent (or great-great-great-parent) box.

Return Statements

Say this is our current code:

```
def func1():
    a = 30
    print(a)
def func2():
    a = 10
    print(a)
a = 5
print(a)
func1()
func2()
```

How would we change the "a" in func2() to become the same as func1()'s "a" without touching the global "a"?

The flowchart on the right depicts a viable way to do so:

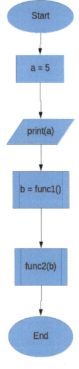

Namespaces and scopes

Our goal here is to **return** the value of "a" in func1() and assign it to another object available in global and then to assign that global variable as a parameter for func2().

This allows us to keep similar names in coexisting scopes but pass them around by essentially renaming the object when it is returned by the function.

Shall we code it?

```python
def func1():
    a = 30
    print(a)
    return a


def func2(b):
    print(b)


a = 5
print(a)
b = func1()
func2(b)
```

The output:

```
5
30

30
```

Classes

This should sound familiar to you if you enjoy "modding" or "hacking" games like Minecraft (I've got a wonderful sister back home who is obsessed over it at the time of writing).

If you go online and search up the term in regard to Python then chances are that your simple blocky mind will be bombarded with fancy terms like "encapsulation of variables and data" or "instances of object holding".

Don't fret little one.

Think of it in this way, classes are a collection of variables and user defined functions which you can use to create a template or a container for your objects. Think of them as your very own structures capable of holding both data and functions. Think of them as objects.

In fact, these are exactly the objects we so repeatedly mentioned alongside the description of Python.

Don't get it? It's perfectly fine to be confused. I was too.

Let's just do an example instead;

Remember the cry() function we made?

Let's make something similar except with a bit more flexibility.

Say we want to input the details of two of the recent victims of Quasimodo, we then have two ways of doing this prior to this chapter:

1) To ask for the victim's details and print out the tombstone text then to loop back again. The downside; output and inputs are mixed making it look messy. That and we must overwrite the previous victim's details. So virtually, it is the same tombstone, just broken and rebuilt again.

2) To tediously assign each person with a variable for each of their information. The downsides; its time consuming and not economical due to the large amount of redundant lines of code.

Classes

And then we have classes. To copy the structure so there can be more than one tombstone, identical only by its capacity to hold and or to process information.

Let's start with one person first.

```python
class tombstone:
    name = ""
    birth = ""
    death = "2018"

    def cry(self):
        print("Rest in pieces {}.\n{} to {}".format(self.name, self.birth, self.death))
# We are now in the main section of the program
person = tombstone() # Assign "template" to this person
person.name = input("Name of victim: ")
person.birth = input("Year of birth: ")
person.cry()
```

In the beginning we defined our class with the name tombstone.

```python
class tombstone:
```

Then we set some variables to it.

```python
name = ""
birth = ""
death = "2018"
```

And don't forget the user defined function!

```python
def cry(self):
    print("Rest in pieces {}.\n{} to {}".format(self.name, self.birth, self.death))
```

The term self here points the interpreter to where it can find the variables to process.

Great! Now we have a "template" (class) which we can copy.

Classes

Now we will assign the "template" to the person (the object in which we want to store and or process data).

```
person = tombstone() # Assign person to this "template"
```

And if we want to manipulate the variables in its "template":

```
person.name = input("Name of victim: ")
person.birth = input("Year of birth: ")
```

We can also do this:

```
person.birth = 1
```

And finally, we call the function defined within it:

```
person.cry()
```

Now if we decide to create a second person too, then our code will end up becoming something like:

```
class tombstone:
    name = ""
    birth = ""
    death = "2018"

    def cry(self):
        print("Rest in pieces {}.\n{} to {}".format(self.name, self.birth, self.death))


# We are now in the main section of the program
# Assign "template" to this person
person = tombstone()
# Assign "template" to this person too
person2 = tombstone()
person.name = input("Name of victim: ")
person.birth = input("Year of birth: ")
person2.name = input("Name of next victim: ")
person2.birth = input("Year of birth: ")
person.cry()
```

And upon execution, you will find that both victims' information are stored separately. They merely copied and followed the structure of our class. Thus, they are identical in operation and shape, but they are not linked to each other.

Let's try to look at this in another way;

Oh, you turned to the next page... I was beginning to think you never would.

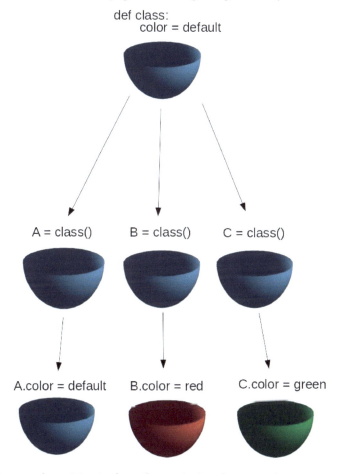

The diagram above tries to show that assigning the same class to several different objects doesn't render them as interdependent.

Loops

Loops are useful for when you want to repeat a segment of code over and over again for as long as a set of conditions are met (It could even go on forever!).

The diagram below tries to give you a basic idea of how loops operate and work:

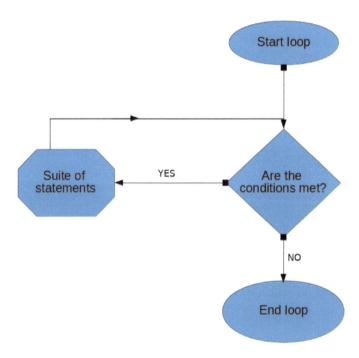

Loops

Done reading?

That was fast... Are you sure you understood the concept?

Let's recap anyways.

A loop can be placed anywhere. They can even be nested within each other (much like the if else statements if you can recall!) and placed virtually anywhere as long as it has a condition (or set of conditions) to meet and fulfill. It first starts by checking if the conditions are fulfilled. From here, it has two possible pathways to choose from. If the conditions are true, then it will execute the suite of statements you wish to be repeated. If the condition(s) are false, then it exits the loop and moves on to the next part of the program whilst merrily singing the Ballad of Mona Lisa...

I made the last part up.

Like all programming languages, Python has loops which programmers can use (duh). Two basic loops to be precise.

1) For loops

2) While loops

For loop

    For loops in Python repeats itself for every element any structure (or sub-structure) provided. This means that if a list is present as a condition in a for loop, the segment of code that is present under the loop structure will be executed and re-executed for every element that exists within the given list. The condition(s) here will be the element(s) present in the ordered structure.

```python
string = "HELLO PYTHON"

for x in string:
    print(x)
```

The output you will get is:

```
H
E
L
L
O

P
Y
T
H
O
N
```

You can even specify sub-structures by slicing like so:

```python
string = "HELLO PYTHON"

for x in string[7:11]:
    print(x)
```

Which gives us:

```
Y
T
H
O
```

See what I did there?

By slicing, we specify that the condition is from the 7th index to the 11th to which Python will then use to repeat the printing process over and over until we reach the 11th index. You get it don't you? Your imagination and creativity to specify the condition is the limit. Go ahead, try reverse printing it. There should be two ways to do it.

We also have a range() function for repeating the for loop for the specified number of times. Below is an example:

```
for x in range(6):
    print(x)
```

Which gives us:

```
0
1
2
3
4
5
```

While loops

The while loop takes a statement or a group of statements as conditions instead of structures (usually mathematical expressions) and will loop over for as long as the conditions are met (I'm getting tired of repeating myself). Simple isn't it? Let's look at an example:

```
number = 1
while number < 10:
    print(number)
    number += 1
```

Which gives us:

```
1
2
3
4
5
6
7
8
9
```

P.S: In case you forgot (again), the while statement in the example above is read as "While variable "number" is less than 10, print the current state of variable number then increment it (Increase value) by 1.". Therefore, 10 does not get printed as 10 is equal to itself and in no way (I hope) less than itself.

But while loops are not confined to only mathematical expressions as conditions, you can even use strings or any other type of changeable structure. Let's try it out using strings.

Loops

Let's try describing how school felt like for me:

```
school = "School was hell"
experience = "School was helllllllllllllllllllllllll"
extra_hell = "l"
while school != experience:
    print(school)
    school = school + extra_hell
```

We have two strings; school and experience.

We want to repeatedly say what school was like until we achieve a satisfactory amount of Ls to match the hellishness of the experience.

Here, we read the while loop as:

"While string school is not equal to string experience, print the current state of school then concentrate string extra_hell with string school."

And to our immense satisfaction, we get:

```
School was hell
School was helll
School was hellll
School was helllll
School was hellllll
School was helllllll
School was hellllllll
School was helllllllll

....

School was helllllllllllllllllllllllll
```

#The rest of the output was cut as it took up too much space.

Although this little experiment of ours was fun and all, it also gave us outputs that were of no use to us and (I admit) a little bit too exaggerated. So, how do we control the loops but at the same time allow them to work in the direction of conditions we had supplied?

Control statements

With control statements, that's what. They allow us to exit or ignore some processes in the loop.

Here's a table:

Control function	Example
continue This will tell the loop to skip the current condition and skip the next iteration.	```number = 1
goal = 669
while number < goal:
if number < 666:
number += 1
continue
print(number)
number += 1``` This will give us an output of: ```666
667
668```
break This allows us to exit the loop even if the condition is true.	```number = 1
goal = 669
while number < goal:
if number < 666:
number += 1
continue
print(number)
break``` This on the other hand gives us: ```666```

Cool isn't it? Now how do we do that to our "school" experiment?

Let's say we want to only print out the final result. But we want to break if L was applied more than 15 times. AND WE WANT THE WHOLE THING TO BE IN CAPS. What should we do then?

Keep in mind that the following example is **NOT** the brightest way to achieve our goal but is to show you how control functions work.

```
school = "School was hell"
experience = "School was hellllllllllllllllllllllllll"
extra_hell = "l"
while school != experience:
    school = school + extra_hell
    for counter in range(15):
        school = school + extra_hell
        continue
    print(school.upper())
    break
    print("This is another statement and will get ignored")
```

As you can see, we have made several changes to the original code. We first used a range() function to repeat the for loop 15 times. And because of that continue statement in the end of the nested loop, we can hope that school doesn't get repeatedly printed as long as L hasn't been applied 15 times. Then we tell Python to print out school after converting all lower case letters to upper cased and exit immediately afterwards. The final statement will get ignored (hopefully) as there is a break statement before it.

Time to execute it.

I don't want to do it.

You do it.

Fine, lets **both** do it.

Ready?

3... 2... 1!!!

```
SCHOOL WAS HELLLLLLLLLLLLLLLLLL
```

Success!

"Synthetic" loops

The two loops described in this chapter are loops we make through the intentional loop holes found in loops (I swear that will be my last crappy joke in this book).

I call them synthetic because we exploit the very nature of loops and use it to our advantage.

Yes, you may call them something else.

You named them what now?

Croissant loops?

That actually not bad.

Wow.

I applaud you.

Infinite loops

These loops will keep repeating itself unless the user terminates it manually. We achieve this by setting a variable that never turns false, never to be touched.

Here is an example:

```
x = 1
while x == 1:
    print(x)
```

Execute the above and you will see ones trailing and stretching into the unknown, farther than Buzz Lightyear can imagine.

Recursive loops

Python allows functions to call themselves in their own body. So, if you were to create a user defined function, you can tell it to call itself again before exiting. Just... Be careful though. If you are not cautious enough, you may end up with an infinite loop or a memory hogging flea (Unless that's what you intend to achieve of course). Below we create a user defined function called recursion()

```python
def recursion(x):
    if x > 0:
        result = x + recursion(x - 1) # Here we call recursion()
        print(result)
    else:
        result = 0
    return result
print("\n\nRecursion:")
recursion(4)
```

The result?

```
Recursion:
0
1
3
6
```

File handling

Being able to read, write and manipulate files opens up an ocean of possibilities to a programmer. And Python couldn't have made it any easier.

Before we head into it, let us first learn to distinguish raw_input() from input(). I'm sure you have been using the latter more often than the first, mostly because I haven't mentioned it up till now (silly me).

raw_input() : Whatever the user enters will be interpreted as a string.

input() : The same as raw_input() except it gets interpreted as a valid expression in Python.

Are we done here?

No?

When will you learn that I am just a book am not capable of caring for another soul.

Now that you have mastered (Not really) the art of reading inputs and writing outputs, let us try and take the next step forward!

For now, keep these two *attributes mode* in mind:

"a" - Means to append to a file. If you recall, appending means to add to.

"w" - Will overwrite the whole file. Yes John, **everything** that have existed before will be replaced with the new input.

"x" - Will create a new file if file does not exist, otherwise it will return an error.

Now, let us take a look at the various methods we can use to manipulate files;

File handling

Method	
open(name, access*, buffering*) Used to open or create new files. Name is the name of the file, access is the *attribute mode* in which you want to access it in. Note that when opening, we need to assign the file to a variable (we call it a file object). This will be useful for when we want to modify it.	`file = open("test.txt", "x")` Output: ▼ ■ **30days** ~/PycharmProjects/30days 　　 🐍 basics.py 　　 📄 test.txt Notice that a new file named test.txt has been created.

close()
 	
 Used for closing a file. You typically need a file to be opened first to close it.
	`file = open("test.txt", "w")`
	 `file.close()`
	
	 File has been closed, you cannot handle it using the file object anymore.

write(string)
 	
 This is used to write in the opened file.
	`f = open("test.txt", "a")`
	 `f.write("Send help, Quasimodo is after me")`
	
	 And when we open test.txt:
	
	 `Send help, Quasimodo is after me`

read(bytes*)
 	
 This will attempt to read the file until the end unless you provide it with the number of bytes it should read.
	`f = open("test.txt", "r")`
	 `print(f.read(9))`
	
	 Which will give us:
	
	 `Send help`

rename(old, new) This will rename the file name if given the current name (old) and the new name you want to give it (new). Note that you need to import the os module and use the os. header instead of the file object. All functions listed in the table after this one is under the OS module.	```import os

os.rename("test.txt", "new.txt")```
 	
Which then changes the file name as seen:
 	
▼ 🗀 **30days** ~/PycharmProjects/30days
   🐍 basics.py
   📄 new.txt
 	
Note that we didn't have to open the file first as the module doesn't need to make use of a file object.

remove(name) This method removes any file when supplied with the file name (name).	```import os
os.remove("new.txt")``` To this you will find your file to seemingly vanish. … Maaagicc (not really).
mkdir(name) mk = make dir= directory This method is used to create new directories.	```import os
os.mkdir("Hello")``` And when you look to your left: ▼ 🗀 **30days** ~/PychamProjects/30days   🗀 Hello

chdir(name) ch = change This method is used when you want to change into another directory. The name argument is the name of the directory	```import os
print(os.getcwd())
os.chdir("Hello")
print(os.getcwd())``` Which gives us an output:
getcwd() cwd = current working directory This method will return the current directory you are in.	/home/marz/PycharmProjects/30days /home/marz/PycharmProjects/30days/H ello We can even change directories with the full path: ```import os
print(os.getcwd())
os.chdir("/home/marz/PycharmProjects
/30days/Hello")
print(os.getcwd())``` Which gives us the same output.
rmdir(name) This function deletes an entire directory (if it is empty!). Name is the name of the directory or the pathway to it.	```import os
os.rmdir("Hello")``` Which gives us: 

Exception handling

Exceptions are events raised by functions when they fail to execute, thus disrupting the seemingly perfect flow of program execution. Exceptions vary by their type and each have their own solutions.

You don't have to learn each and every type of exception at the current moment. At least, it won't be necessary to until you encounter them. But what do you do when you get an exception? Do you change your source code drastically? Or do you keep trying?
If you answered anything but the latter, get out of my sight.

Say we have the following code:

```
f = open("testfile", "x")
f.write("This is an example of exception handling!!")
print("Written content in the file successfully")
```

You should be able to understand what it means. And recall that if the file is already existing, then "x" would raise an exception. So, run it twice to get the error:

```
f = open("testfile", "x")
FileExistsError: [Errno 17] File exists: 'testfile'
```

A simple DuckDuckGo search and research gives us the information that this is a form of IOError which typically rises when there are errors related to input and output operations.

Hence, we can use try, except and finally statements to try and handle these exceptions.

Statement	Description
try	When expecting an exception, use the try statement then nest the trouble-making segments of code in it
except	This will be called in the case where the specified exception gets raised
else	This will be called if the except statement does not get called.

```python
try:
    f = open("testfile", "x")
    f.write("This is an example of exception handling!!")
except IOError:
    print("Error: can\'t open file. It exists")
else:
    print("Written content in the file successfully")
    f.close()
```

Which at first gives us:

Written content in the file successfully

Along with a successful creation of the "test" file.

But when executed again;

Error: can't open file. It exists

Nicely done!

Finally statement

The segment of code that follows it will get executed no matter what. Exception or not, "finally" will have the final laugh.

We can experiment by doing;

```
try:
    f = open("testfile", "x")
    f.write("This is an example of exception handling!!")
except IOError:
    print("Error: can\'t open file. It exists")
else:
    print("Written content in the file successfully")
    f.close()
finally:
    print("Goodbye")
```

Just to find that that we will be bade farewell by the program no matter the outcome of the tries and excepts.

Our big project

Now that we know the principles to coding a full-fledged application, let us embark on a quest!

Oh look!

There comes zombie John and zombie Adam!

Uh, John... Where's your-

Never mind.

See?!

They are all so excited to do something that they would even come back from the dead for the glory.

The task

Design a number guessing game with the following features:

> 1) Point system complete with win streak rewarding.

> 2) Scoreboard.

> 3) Print the total scores to a specified txt file if wanted.

> 4) Maximum of 10 players and minimum of 2

You ready to pretend like you're in the real world?

Great!

> Why do I feel like I run a popular kids' show that teaches a foreign language while trying to cram in shitty philosophy?

Oh.

Well it's too late to rewrite the book now...

Our big project

We can already see that we have four main parts which we must code to make this game a success:

- A menu function

- A game function

- A scoreboard

- Exporting files

Since we have been given a list of things needed to be done, let's try to create a generalized flowchart to get a basic idea of what we might need.

Seems simple right?

Let's get to work.

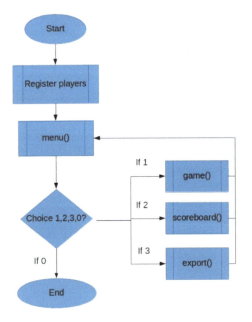

Reader, you can oversee coding the menu and player registration.

And since your part is so easy to code, you can later assist Quasimodo with the game, John with the scoreboard and then Adam with the exporting features after you are done.

Too much work?

I simply don't care.

register()

The menu function should print the menu then ask the user to input a choice and would finally direct the program to the

You called for me? You're having trouble with scripting the menu you say? What's so hard about it? Did you at least sketch a flowchart for it? Oh, you did.

You see, there's a problem on the very beginning of your flowchart, you've defined player name as a set, when sets aren't ordered or indexed, this will cause troubles when you try to align it with the player's scores. Your best bet is by creating a list since it can hold several strings in one place while retaining the changeable, ordered, and indexed attributes.

Our big project

Thus, if our code where to follow your flowchart, it would look something like:

```
def register():

    player_name = list()
    play_count = 0
    counter = int(input("How many players are there? (1-10): "))
    if counter < 2:
        print("Error: There must be more than two players!")
        register()


    elif counter > 10:
        print("Error: There must be less than 10 players!")
        register()
    while play_count != counter:
        player_name.append(input(str("Enter Player {}'s name: ".format(play_count + 1))))
        play_count += 1
    return counter, player_name
```

We have to return the counter and the player_name list so that other functions can make use of them.

As you can imagine, the counter will be especially useful in places where they need to count the max number of turns they will give in total to the players whereas the player_name list will be crucial when printing out the scoreboard or in places where we would like to refer to the player by name.

Therefore, our first main segment now looks likes:

```
counter, players = register()

menu()
```

menu()

Now for the menu;

This one is so simple, that creating a flowchart isn't necessary at all.

Our task is simple:

1) Print out menu options

2) Get player choice

3) Use if else statements to handle direction of program flow

```
scores = [0, 0, 0, 0, 0, 0, 0, 0, 0, 0]


def menu(scores):
    print("\t\n\tWelcome to the numbers guessing game!\n\n")
    print("1. Play the game")
    print("2. Scoreboard")
    print("3. Print scores to a .txt file")
    print("0. Exit\n\n")
    choice = int(input("Choice (0-3): "))
    if choice == 0:
        exit()
    elif choice == 1:
        scores = game(scores)
        score(scores)
    elif choice == 2:
        score(scores)
    elif choice == 3:
        export(scores)
    else:
        print("Invalid choice!")
    menu(scores)
```

Notice that we added a global score list so it can be accessed from any other internal scope. Now shoo. Go help Quasimodo with the game

And remember to bring along a notebook with you for modifications to menu() and register() might be necessary.

game()

Bonjour! I am Quasimodo! ⊂(◉‿◉)つ

So, Monsieur Marzouq has sent you to help me, is it not? Tsk tsk.

You have gotten the cockroaches no? Ah, you are surprised? It is something we say when someone is feeling down, "Avoir le cafard".

You are laughing.

Why are you laughing? •̆) •̆

Do not take them lightly my friend! They are plotting to overthrow us all! Mark my word!

Anyway, I am becoming a goat because of this piece of code Monsieur Marzouq has asked me to finish. It is impossible to generate a random number in the range of 0-10 properly! Here, have a look at flowchart I made before fixing the code that has been cursed!

As you can see, I have planned the out of everything very carefully.

All I have trouble with is the random number generation.

To make thing even worse, I do not have connection to the Internet!

Our big project

The situation is not as bad you say?

What can possibly top this?

Pineapples on pizza? WHO HAS MADE SUCH A THING?! ┳┳ ⌒ /(.□. \)

If that is what the future holds I swear on my baguettes that I will behead each and every one who dares to enjoy such an atrocity!

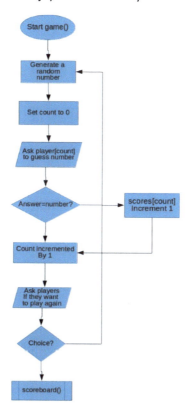

Our big project

Here is the code I have so far:

```python
def game(scores):
    #insert generator here
    count = 0
    while count != counter:
        ans = int(input("{}, guess the number! (0-10): ".format(players[count])))
        if ans == random_num:
            scores[count] += 10
        count += 1
    print("And the correct number was: {}".format(random_num))
    choice = input('Press "y" to play again:')
    if choice == "y" or choice == "Y":
        game(scores)

    else:
        print("\n\n\n\n\n")
        score(scores)
```

What do the we do now? I have heavily depended on the internet up till now...

What is that? You have an idea? Fast now! Share it!

Ah!

I see you have used the help() function in the python interpreter to search for the random module!

Very smart indeed!

Let us first try creating pseudo-codes to test them out.

You do not know how to use pseudo-codes my friend? Not of worries!

```
Help on module random:

NAME
    random - Random variable generators.

MODULE REFERENCE
    https://docs.python.org/3.5/library/random.html

    The following documentation is automatically generated from the Python
    source files.  It may be incomplete, incorrect or include features that
    are considered implementation detail and may vary between Python
    implementations.  When in doubt, consult the module reference at the
    location listed above.

DESCRIPTION
    integers
    --------
            uniform within range

    sequences
    ---------
            pick random element
            pick random sample
            generate random permutation

    distributions on the real line:
    ------------------------------
            uniform
            triangular
            normal (Gaussian)
            lognormal
            negative exponential
            gamma
            beta
```

I am of owings you some secrets anyways...

Just drop into the python interpreter and code away statements like so:

Oh no...

```
>>> from random import random
>>> number = random()
>>> print(number)
0.37866051945167656
>>>
```

It seemings that the number generator is generating numbers from 0 to 1!

We need one that can generate from 0 to 10!

Multiply by 10? But that would just give us 5.811 and a bunch of other numbers trailing it! How would we then compare it?

I think I haved gotten it! Let us round them off after multiplying!

And if I use your trick then I will surely find such a rounding off function of sorts!

```
Help on built-in function round in module builtins:

round(...)
    round(number[, ndigits]) -> number

    Round a number to a given precision in decimal digits (default 0 digits).
    This returns an int when called with one argument, otherwise the
    same type as the number. ndigits may be negative.
(END)
```

Viola!

Now back to our pseudo-code!

```
>>> from random import random
>>> number = random()
>>> print(number)
0.37866051945167656
>>> number = number*10
>>> number = round(number)
>>> print(number)
4
```

ZUT ALORS! THAT WORKED! Now to put it in the main program!

Thank you for your assistance monsieur. You can go now. You are offended?

What do you mean I can't just assume your gender in 2018?

I think I prefer the year of terror more than yours now...

scoreboard()

John here!   (╥﹏╥)

So, you've finished helping the old geezer with the game huh?

Well that's great cause I'm gonna need you to tell me how the player names and scores are stored to able to print them out in the first place.

There's the flowchart.

Pick it up will ya? My last arm fell off just as I finished prototyping the scoreboard. Being an undead has its difficulties.

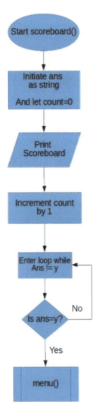

Our big project

And there's the code, have fun reading, I'm off to get some Dunkin' Donuts:

```python
def scoreboard(score):
    count = 0
    print("Scores for the game!")
    print('--------------------')
    while count != counter:
        print("%-14s|%-14i" % (player_name[count],
player_scores[count]))
        print('--------------------')
        count += 1
    menu(scores)
```

Annnnnnd I'm back (つ ´⌣`ς)! You've made changes accordingly?

Lemme see!

```python
def score(scores):
    count = 0
    print("Scores for the game!")
    print('--------------------')
    while count != counter:
        print("%-14s|%-14i" % (players[count], scores[count]))
        print('--------------------')
        count += 1
    menu(scores)
```

Hah! I wasn't far off now, was I? I ask the baguette lover for a peak at his code so I knew what I was doing.

```python
print("%-14s|%-14i" % (players[count], scores[count]))
```

You don't understand the printing format? Here, let Johnny teach you a thing or two about the 'Murican way.

Our big project

You see, I hate Marzouq's way of printing. I prefer the old ways when things were much simpler, and you could use '%' to do everything.

Here's the statement broken down:

14	Space given to the output
-	left align
s	Stands for string
i	Integer

Smart, aren't I?

Gotta thank Uncle Sam for these brains.

Anyways, I gotta bounce and find some brain burgers or something...

See ya!

export()

Don't you dang kids know how to knock? ಠ_ಠ

What's that? You're here to yelp?

There is absolutely no need for such randomness young one!

Speak up will you!?

For Jericho's sake, stop mumbling!
Oh! You are here to help good old Adam is it?! Marvelous!

You see, whenever the user types in the name of a file that is already existing, then I get some sort of an error;

```
FileExistsError: [Errno 17] File exists: 'testfile'
```

I also get weird outputs for the exporting:

```
|Scores for the game!|---------------------|ads ...
```

You would like to see my code? Well, by all means;

```python
def export(scores):
    filename = input("Name of file:")
    filename = filename + '.txt'
    f = open(filename, "x")
    f = open(filename, "a")
    count = 0
    f.write("|Scores for the game!|")
    f.write("---------------------")
    while count != counter:
        f.write("|%-12s|%-12i" % (players[count], scores[count]))
        f.write("---------------------")
        count += 1
```

Ah, I see you are already working on fixing it! You have found the problem I suppose?

Our big project

Fun? No, I am NOT having fun! You kids smell weird nowadays! Run?! Is it the chubby raptor again? Give me a club and let me at him then! Oh... you're done.

Well then, what are you waiting for?! Show me! I'm not getting younger anytime soon!

```python
def export(scores):
    filename = input("Name of file:")
    filename = filename + '.txt'
    try:
        f = open(filename, "x")
        f = open(filename, "a")
    except IOError:
        f = open(filename, "a")
    count = 0
    f.write("|Scores for the game!|\n")
    f.write("--------------------\n")
    while count != counter:
        f.write("|%-12s|%-12i\n" % (players[count], scores[count]))
        f.write("--------------------\n")
        count += 1
    menu(scores)
```

Why... THAT WORKS!
YOU'RE A GENIUS!

I thank you for your services dear child.

(ಠ ﮌ ಠ)

Finishing up

So, you've finished helping out the others in coding their parts of the program? Good. Now, you need to iron out the bugs and make sure the program isn't faulty. Some of the few things you can do is to apply exception handlers where we expect the player to make mistakes and to make sure the program goes on smoothly.

For instance, I took the liberty of fool-proofing the game() function by adding exception handlers and a range:

```python
def game(scores):
    random_num = random()
    random_num *= 10; random_num = round(random_num)
    count = 0
    while count != counter:
        ans = int(input("{}, guess the number! (0-10): ".format(players[count])))
        try:
            if ans == random_num:
                scores[count] += 10
            elif ans > 10 or ans < 0:
                print("Out of range! Moving on!")
        except IOError:
            print("Error! Must be an integer!")
        count += 1
    print("And the correct number was: {}".format(random_num))
    choice = input('Press "y" to play again:')
    if choice == "y" or choice == "Y":
        game(scores)
    else:
        print("\n\n\n\n\n")
        score(scores)
```

Testing

Let's try testing out the game before shipping it off to our clients.

This stage is crucial as you can imagine in ensuring that everything would work as planned.

```
How many players are there? (1 - 10): 2
Enter Player1's name: Sad B O I I
Enter Player2's name: b0ss


            Welcome to the numbers guessing game!


1. Play the game
2. Scoreboard
3. Print scores to a .txt file
0. Exit

Choice(0 - 3): 1
Sad B O I I, guess the number! (0 - 10): 2
b0ss, guess the number! (0 - 10): 3
And the correct number was: 10

Press "y"to play again: y

....
And the correct number was: 8

Press "y" to play again: n

Scores for the game!
--------------------
Sad B O I I| 10
--------------------
b0ss         | 0
--------------------
```

```
                Welcome to the numbers guessing game!

1. Play the game
2. Scoreboard
3. Print scores to a .txt file
0. Exit

Choice(0 - 3): 2
Scores for the game!
--------------------
Sad B O I I | 10
--------------------
b0ss            | 0
--------------------

                Welcome to the numbers guessing game!

1. Play the game
2. Scoreboard
3. Print scores to a .txt file
0. Exit

Choice(0 - 3): 4
Invalid choice!

                Welcome to the numbers guessing game!

1. Play the game
2. Scoreboard
3. Print scores to a .txt file
0. Exit

Choice(0 - 3): 3
Name of file: hi
# Here we can see a file being created.

                Welcome to the numbers guessing game!
```

```
....
Choice(0 - 3): 0
```

Seems like everything's perfect doesn't it?

I won't lie, it does seem to do everything as advertised.

But the development cycle doesn't end there. In the near future, you will find the need to add new features, eye-candies and functions.

For instance, you might find that printing "Scores successfully exported!" after finishing the export will make the program feel more human and friendly and less calculative and cold.

What's my point in telling you this?

Always write your program in a flexible way and make sure there is extensive documentation so anyone developing it in the future will know exactly what they are doing.

But as far as you are concerned, you have kept your end of the deal. All that matters now is that if it works and if you followed the work ethic by documenting your code.

Happily ever after...

Take a bow, you are now a full-fledged developer.

Are you done pumping your fists?

Good.

Now for the hard part. (ÒдÓ́ᵔ)

And before you start questioning me why I am just now moving to the hard part of programming when the book is nearing to its end, it is because programming isn't hard when you learn it.

At least not **as** hard. ┬──┬ ╱(˚- ˚╱)

In fact, this is the most fun you will get out of it; the learning and exploration of the abstract mathematical world that comes alive along with the grand tango between a human mind and a Python's.

The hard part comes when everything seems theoretically flawless but fails nonetheless. This is where your mastery of the art of programming comes into play.

Mastery of programming can never be achieved through the memorization of documentation. In fact, if the thought of mastering it through memorization of this book occurred to you at all, then I consider you to be a humongous fool.

There are three reasons for this:

1) Programming languages are ever evolving. Chances are that when you buy this book, a newer version of Python is available and you are now equipped with an outdated memory of tables (that is if you gained mastery through memorizing instead of trying to gain understanding).

2) Programming does not start and end with Python. You may have bought this book so you can go out into the world and call yourself a Python programmer, but I am here to tell you that striving to be a master of only one language is something very short sighted. Say hypothetically, you are given the

opportunity to earn a few million bucks if you programmed a simple Java application. And it HAS to be in Java because Python in this hypothetical world is now a forgotten fossil. Would you give up? Would you learn how to program all over again? Both choices are stupid.

3) This book does not teach you the advanced folds of programming. It barely teaches you the basics!

Now, before you start getting ready to drag yourself to my doorstep along with an angry mob, I have two things to say.

One, I have a Quasimodo.   ℃(° ⊠ʃ °)Ɔ

And two, you have gained something far more valuable than learning how to regurgitate blocks for suites to achieve something. You have gained understanding of how your Python thinks. And as it grows and gets much more advanced, you will find that adapting to the ever-evolving world is easier as you know exactly what to do and where to go.

And that is why I wrote this book.

You see, I was once a young new Python trainer like you. I remember how impossible it seemed to learn how to one day learn how to type in colorful streaks of statements that would later be understood and obeyed by magnificent and fascinating machines.

The thought of being able to communicate with an entity so differently intelligent overwhelmed me.

"Can I really do it?"

Formal and lengthy textbooks did nothing but discourage me and frustrate me with the idea that programming was only for those who were mathematically intelligent. (° ʃ °)

No.

Programming was for anyone capable of communicating and solving puzzles.

It is for people with willpower and vision.

The language itself is our bridge to communicating and directing the mathematical geniuses that rule today's virtual world.

Computers.

And you are now their complete master, never forget that. (■_■)

The sheer motivation alone and the stress it takes for your constantly evolving carbon-based brain to understand this peculiar and undefined world is something very few succeed in doing.

Again, congratulations for that. ๑_๑

I am truly honored and humbled to be a part of the journey that you are now taking to become a Python trainer.
And thus, I shall end this chapter and book by wishing you luck, farewell and a few parting words;

The mastery of language itself sparks innovations and revolutions.

Glossary

argument

A value passed to a function (or method) when calling the function.

attribute

A value associated with an object which is referenced by name using dotted expressions. For example, if an object o has an attribute a it would be referenced as o.a.

class

A template for creating user-defined objects. Class definitions normally contain method definitions which operate on instances of the class.

code

The language that programmers use to tell the computer what to do.

command

Instructions for the computer.

data

Information. Often inputs and outputs of programs.

debugging

Finding and fixing problems in a program.

dictionary

An associative array, where arbitrary keys are mapped to values. The keys can be any object with __hash__() and __eq__() methods. Called a hash in Perl.

file object

An object exposing a file-oriented API (with methods such as read() or write()) to an underlying resource. Depending on the way it was created, a file object can mediate access to a real on-disk file or to another type of storage or communication device (for example standard input/output, in-memory buffers, sockets, pipes, etc.). File objects are also called file-like objects or streams.

for loops

A loop with a given beginning, ending and step interval.

function

A series of statements which returns some value to a caller. It can also be passed zero or more arguments which may be used in the execution of the body. See also parameter, method, and the Function definitions section.

importing

The process by which Python code in one module is made available to Python code in another module.

iteration

A repetitive action usually created in loops.

list

A built-in Python sequence. Despite its name it is more akin to an array in other languages than to a linked list since access to elements is O(1).

loop

The action of doing something over and over again.

method

A function which is defined inside a class body. If called as an attribute of an instance of that class, the method will get the instance object as its first argument (which is usually called self). See function and nested scope.

module

An object that serves as an organizational unit of Python code. Modules have a namespace containing arbitrary Python objects. Modules are loaded into Python by the process of importing.

namespace

The place where a variable is stored. Namespaces are implemented as dictionaries. There are the local, global and built-in namespaces as well as nested namespaces in objects (in methods). Namespaces support modularity by preventing naming conflicts. For instance, the functions builtins.open and os.open() are distinguished by their namespaces. Namespaces also aid readability and maintainability by making it clear which module implements a function. For instance, writing random.seed() or itertools.islice() makes it clear that those functions are implemented by the random and itertools modules, respectively.

online

To be connected to the internet.

output

The information presented when interfacing with hardware.

Package

A Python module which can contain submodules or recursively, sub packages. Technically, a package is a Python module with an __path__ attribute.

parameter

A named entity in a function (or method) definition that specifies an argument (or in some cases, arguments) that the function can accept.

program

A set of statements to be run by a computer.

programming

The process of creating a program.

statement

A statement is part of a suite (a "block" of code). A statement is either an expression or one of several constructs with a keyword, such as if, while or for.

type

The type of a Python object determines what kind of object it is; every object has a type. An object's type is accessible as its __class__ attribute or can be retrieved with type(obj).

variable

A placeholder for information.

virtual environment

A cooperatively isolated runtime environment that allows Python users and applications to install and upgrade Python distribution packages without interfering with the behaviour of other Python applications running on the same system.

while loop

A loop that will repeat as long as condition is true.

Zen of Python

Listing of Python design principles and philosophies that are helpful in understanding and using the language. The listing can be found by typing "import this" at the interactive prompt.

Index

About the author.

At the time of writing, Marzouq Abedur Rahman is an 18-year-old college student of the International Islamic University of Malaysia.

His love of programming started at the age of 12 when he first joined a robotics club during his secondary years and went on to win several gold medals in two separate international robotics championships.

Aside from participating in robotics competitions, he has developed mobile apps, neural networks and cyber security related applications.

He aims to prove the world that programming is for everyone and anyone capable of reading and writing.

He hates formalities and is often quite the comedian (though his humor gets bland at times).

He is also an artist who goes under the pen-name "Natsukashi".

Don't believe me?

WELL TOO BA-I mean; thanks for reading my crappy book!   (~¯▽¯)~

www.ingramcontent.com/pod-product-compliance
Lightning Source LLC
Chambersburg PA
CBHW041154050326

40690CB00004B/556